No ORDINARY Soldier

A Spiritual Survival Guide
of Faith, Hope, and Love

JAMILLAH MCCLENDON LYNN

Book Cover Design: Prize Publishing House

Printed by: Prize Publishing House, LLC in the United States of America.

First printing edition 2022.

Prize Publishing House
P.O. Box 9856, Chesapeake, VA 23321
www.PrizePublishingHouse.com

ISBN (Paperback): 979-8-9862969-3-7
ISBN (E-Book): 979-8-9862969-4-4

Library of Congress Control Number: 2022913757

DEDICATION

This book is dedicated to:

Commander in Chief Edriece

My husband, Edriece, you have been my rock and shield, guarding my heart, loving me unconditionally, and doing an exceptional job of showing our children what a father looks like. The way you love me is proof that God is real. You know me more than anyone in this world, and I love doing life with you.

Drill Sergeant Bobbie McClendon

You raised and trained me to maneuver through life's obstacle course. There are so many words to describe you. Being kind, loving, strong, and encouraging stand out the most. Thank you for showing me how to take pride in everything I do. I love you, Mom.

Specialist Imari

You started as my little sweet pea, and God has blessed you to blossom into such a bright and beautiful butterfly. You give me life with every beat of your golden heart. I can genuinely say that you are my favorite singer, dancer, writer, and female artist. I pray that you never second guess yourself. The sky is the limit for you.

Corporal Junior

It's no wonder you are named after your father because you help me stay in step. I don't miss a beat with you around. You amaze me with your technological skills. You show me that you can do anything you put your mind to. I never tire of seeing your bright "SONshine." You make even the darkest moments appear "SONny side up!" As you walk with God, I pray that He guides your footsteps into a world of adventure.

Private First Class Eric

Eric, you make me feel so important and beautiful. Thank you for always complimenting me, making me laugh, and putting up with me as your homeschool teacher for nearly three years. Your name means "leader." Continue to lead by example. I love you, Buddy.

Private Ella

You were a soldier, even in the womb. You continued to fight to survive against all odds. Your first name has the same meaning as my name – beautiful. Your middle name (Ma'Ry) means "beloved" and "wished for child." You are named after both me and your father's maternal grand-mothers. That is why you are such a wonderful addition to our family. My "wished for" child, I love you so much. You have inspired me to believe in the impossible. My prayer is that you soar to the highest of heights.

IN LOVING MEMORY

-Fallen Soldiers-

My maternal grandparents, T.C. and Mary Smith
My paternal grandmother, Glendora McClendon
My godmother, Lucille Hailey
My uncle and aunt, Noah and Doris Richardson
My spiritual parents, Dr. Purvis and Ruth Givens
My cheerleaders, Cheloy Walker and Francine Williams
My former principals, Vicki Patterson and Gloria Luster
My friends, Yulinda Liggins and Betty Johnson
My heart, Terry Wilson-Lee

ACKNOWLEDGEMENTS

I thank God for trusting me with this journey. Without Him, I could not have navigated through all the twists, turns, ups, and downs life had to offer. He is my reason for living, giving my life new meaning. I also appreciate Him for the ones He carefully placed in my life. I wish to extend my sincere thanks to my "only begotten sister," Katrina. Thank you for making me laugh when I felt like crying and for all the sacrifices you made for me. To my battle buddy in Ft. Stewart, Tawana, you not only picked me up on the battlefield but encouraged me to be a soldier off the battlefield.

Finally, I salute everyone who has been a part of my life. You know who you are. Your name may not be written in this book, but it is written in my heart.

INTRODUCTION

My life is my story. This book is designed to help shed light on the making of me by sharing my upbringing and areas where I see the handprint of God over my life. Each chapter is a highlighted moment that helped prepare me for God's greater purpose.

Since God is the author and finisher of our faith, my prayer is that my story will inspire you to trust the process of becoming who you are destined to be. I want to inspire you by being proof that you can live a good life even when being dealt a bad hand. Be patient and give God time to work in your life. He is still writing your story. Every chapter (the good, bad, and ugly) is vitally important. You'll learn to feel better about the hard parts of your life when you realize hardships often prepare everyday people for an extraordinary destiny.

19 Seventy-Five

What was so unusual about July 11, 1975? Though it may not be such a special day, it was a unique year.

I was born on a hot, sunny afternoon in Phoenix, Arizona. There was nothing unusual about this particular day in July, except that it was on a Friday. Fridays are thought to be a special day of the week. I have heard people say, "I can't wait 'til Friday comes!" When this last day of the work week arrives, people shout, "Thank God it's Friday!" In addition, some consider the numbers seven and eleven lucky numbers. Those with strong beliefs consider seven to be God's number of completion. These numbers really shine when they are celebrated on a Friday. It is a day when most people get paid. For my mother and father, they hit the jackpot with the arrival of their second baby girl—me!

I don't know how it is in everyone else's family, but for mine, when a child is born, they ask two common questions and three when it's a girl: *Who does she look like? How much does she weigh? Does she have any hair?*

I didn't look like my mother or father. I resembled my aunt on my dad's side. To me, the fact that I didn't weigh seven pounds and some change, but precisely seven pounds, is very unusual. I was a caramel baby with a few strands of hair, which my mom would try to slick down with baby lotion. I was definitely baldheaded. I came out darker than anyone in my family, born in the 7th month on the 11th day, weighing precisely seven pounds. Wow!

I was no ordinary baby. My parents named me Jamillah (Juh-mill-uh), which means "beautiful." It also means elegant, graceful, lovely, and comely. If you were to ask my sister or cousins, they would tell you that I was none of these things growing up. I wish someone had told me, or even them, that it would take years and decades before I would be considered the full definition of my name.

NO ORDINARY APPETITE – HUNGER PAINS

I was told I came out of the womb crying. It began when a loud noise echoed from the nursery. Inquiries of *whose baby is that* circulated throughout the hospital. My own mother questioned, "Whose child is screaming like that from the top of their lungs?" She soon received her answer when the nurse walked into her room, carrying me with my mouth wide open and screaming with a piercing cry. Every single ounce of me was more than ready to be fed. The nurses tried to give me a pacifier. I was not having it. They even tried giving me a bottle of what they called back in the day "sugar water." Whatever it was, it was not the solution I was looking for. I wanted my mommy. The nurses and everyone on staff thanked God it was Friday and that my mom chose to breastfeed me. Not too long after she nursed me, I was hungry for more. This hunger pattern followed me throughout my life.

19 Seventy-Six... (almost)

No one holds on tighter than someone who refuses to let go. There's nothing wrong with fighting for what you trust is yours. At least that's what I believed at nine months old. I had so much determination and persistence that I stopped at nothing to achieve my goals. This was the year God developed my strength. Of course, I was too young to realize it, but God blessed me to build muscle and develop a tight grip. I learned early how to hold on no matter what.

My mother had bought my sister a little toy puppy named "Sherlock." It was a white and brown wooden Weiner dog with long, floppy ears. It was about the height and length of an average shoe box. It had four red wheels and a string in which to pull it. Whenever my sister would pull the string, the tail would wiggle and waggle. According to the babysitter, I would watch her do this repeatedly and was amazed. The babysitter noticed my excitement and asked my sister to bring the dog close so I could touch it. To her surprise, I immediately grabbed the tail and pulled it. My sister pulled. I pulled some more. My sister eventually let go after the babysitter told her to let me play with it. Unfortunately, when she did, the dog went flying and conked me directly in the middle of my right eyebrow, cutting it wide open.

It wasn't the blood everywhere that caused the babysitter to panic. It wasn't even the look of shock on my sister's face. It was the noise coming out of my mouth. I had no ordinary cry. My mom described how I would have my mouth wide open without a peep coming out at first. It was because I was holding my breath. Then, after about thirty seconds or so, I would let out a sound piercing to the soul, just like I did when I was first born.

My poor babysitter didn't know what to do. She did what anyone else would do in her situation—she called my mom to come to the rescue.

19 Seventy-Nine

> "Ask and it will be given to you; seek and you will find; knock and the door will be opened to you."
>
> — [MATTHEW 7:7] —

It's true that "closed mouths don't get fed." That's why I couldn't blame anyone else for not exercising my voice. I learned in this year how to open wide.

At this age, I knew *how* to talk; I just chose *not* to talk. Instead, (according to my mother), I would point and expect everyone around me to know exactly what I wanted. It was like a guessing game. They would guess until I shook my head, *"Yes!"*

One day, after my mother had dropped me off on her way to work, she turned around because she had forgotten something. I was a child who was always hungry. I mean, who doesn't get an appetite when they're over at their grandma's house? To top things off, my grandmother was frying my all-time favorite—chicken. My mom's youngest sibling, Uncle Ricky, was there to witness this dramatic event.

"Do you want this, Nuke?" asked my grandma.

I shook my head, *"No!"*

"I think she wants this. Do you want some chicken, Nuke?" asked my uncle.

Before I could fix my head to nod, *"Yes,"* my mom came through the door and asked, "What are y'all doing? Jamillah knows how to talk." She looked at me and said, "You better start opening your mouth and asking for what you want. And you're not getting any chicken until you ask for it!" Turning aside to look at my uncle and grandmother, she demanded, "Do NOT give her any chicken unless she opens her mouth and asks for it!"

Those words were torturous as she left. That is way too much pressure to put on a four-year-old's shoulders. I was Jamillah or Nuke (short for "Nuka," which was even shorter for "Nugget," but that's not important). I was to be treated special. Granted, I wasn't a baby, but being the youngest granddaughter (at the time) gave room for a little spoiling.

Even though I was no ordinary child, I was wrong! My Uncle Ricky cried tears of laughter as he explained how I continuously left out the kitchen and ran into the den three or four times with tears in my eyes. On the last go-'round, I returned with a bag full of determination and yelled, "I … want… some… CHICKEN!!!"

NO ORDINARY PRE-SCHOOLER

Later this year, I exercised this gift of opening wide to my pre-school teacher. Since I only had her for a half day, I did my best to help fulfill her day with my continuous hand raises, taps on the leg, and constant blurt-outs of the all-time favorite "Teacher, Teacher!" Even if she was irritated with me and the other 19 or so students, she never showed it on her face.

I enjoyed playing in Pre-K, well, except when she tried to teach me how to cut. I was no ordinary preschooler. I was left-handed. I needed my own desk with lots of space and special scissors. I loved how I would get my scissors first. The unique pair was designed perfectly to make my cutting experience enjoyable. It was all about me.

"Would you like to pass out everyone else's, Jamillah?" she said insistently.

"Jamillah?" I thought to myself. *"My name is 'Nuka.'"* No one in my family called me "Jamillah." I didn't realize it was a nickname.

I never turned down an opportunity to help the teacher because, at the end of the day, she was my "snack dealer." She would give me all the leftover snacks and cartons of milk everyone else didn't eat or drink. It was like heaven on earth. It worked out great until she ruined it.

"Mrs. Florez, is it okay if we send someone to escort Jamillah down to the principal's office?" the school secretary buzzed over the classroom intercom.

"Sure, that'll be fine. Jamillah, go stand by the door," Mrs. Florez directed.

I had no idea what I had done to be beckoned to the principal's office, but I was eager to find out.

"Jamillah, do you know why you're here?" asked the principal.

I shook my head, *"No."*

"I want to ask you a couple of questions. Is that okay?"
I nodded, *"Yes."*

"Who do you live with?" she asked.

"My mommy and sister."

"Do you have food to eat at home? Does your mommy fix it for you?" she continued.

"Yes!" I said with an enormous grin on my face. I loved the very mention of food.

"Okay, I'm going to have someone walk you back to class," she said.

On my way out, I saw my sister and my cousin. They were sitting in the chair, waiting to get questioned too. So, I did what I always did whenever I saw my family—I smiled, waved, and let everyone else know who they were.

I found out later they were called down to see the principal and why my mom was called at work. My teacher was concerned about my nutrition and told the principal I always asked for other classmates' snacks.

My mother didn't get upset. Instead, she requested that the principal ask my sister and cousin. The principal received all the proof she needed when my cousin and sister both said, "Yes, and she always asks for the *mostest!*"

I constantly stayed hungry. It wasn't because I didn't get fed. For as long as I could remember, my mom never failed to make us a hot breakfast and pack us a nice lunch. I just took advantage of the opportunity to eat again once I got to school. It wasn't my fault that I was a bottomless pit.

19 Eighty-One

NO ORDINARY MOVE - LET GO AND LET GOD

"Brethren, I count not myself to have apprehended: but this one thing I do, forgetting those things which are behind, and reaching forth unto those things which are before."

— [PHILIPPIANS 3:13] —

A person never fully realizes the weight of something they've been holding until they let it go. This was the year I discovered that I couldn't hold onto everything. I learned early how to let some things and people go.

In my opinion, every little girl is a father's princess. She looks up to him because a dad is a girl's first hero. He's the one that will pick her up when mommy says, "Be a big girl." He's the one who fights off the monsters in bad dreams or throws you up high in the air and catches you before you fall. That is exactly what my father was to me. He would read my sister and me bedtime stories every night before we went to sleep. These weren't your ordinary stories—they were ones he had made up or put together from a combination of other familiar stories. For instance, instead of *Goldilocks and the Three Bears*, he would name it *Little Nuke and the Three Cupcakes*. Each story was animated and humorous. The way he ended them always left you wanting for more.

When he and my mom divorced, my mom moved back to Flint, Michigan, to start anew. I didn't understand why we couldn't see my dad every day or why the bedtime stories had to be told over the phone. I missed my dad. I wanted him to come back.

As time passed, I recall my mom taking my sister and me to the mall. While inside, we held her hands as we window shopped. "Mom! Look! It's Daddy! Daddy?" My sister and I spotted our father at the mall. He was with a woman I didn't recognize. I couldn't understand why he pretended not to know us.

"Daddy?" I repeated as I let go of my mother's hand and ran to him. My hero turned and walked away.

I envisioned him scooping us up like he used to, swinging us around and telling us how pretty we were. To our surprise, he didn't even recognize us (at least that's what he led us to believe). He left us standing there, crying, and confused. Even years after their divorce, nothing but God could fill the void he left inside, especially when my dad was yet alive.

My mom held us both, wiped our tears, and encouraged us to hold onto her hand. I didn't look back. I chose to look forward. It was healing. It was hopeful. Eventually, letting go was freeing.

19 Eighty-Three

I f I could talk to my younger self, I would say, "Learn who you are. Embrace yourself. Explore the world and find your own flavor." These things are so vital because, too often, we try to find ourselves by pleasing others. It's important that we find our own style and free ourselves from people's opinions.

During this year, God showed me how to dress myself. It's not necessarily what you wear, but what you put on. Yes, my mom taught me how to properly put on natural attire – like my shoes and clothes. I knew not to wear dirty underwear or mismatched socks. God taught me how to put on happiness in times of sorrow, peace in the midst of confusion, and faith whenever fear was present. He also revealed to me what *not* to wear.

My mom was always one who acted her wage. She didn't dress us in the latest fashions just to keep up with the Joneses. She did what she could when she could, and how she could. She would make us different outfits in which we would wear our clothes two days in a row. As we got older, we would alternate items on certain days of the week.

It was no ordinary schedule. Whatever I wore on Monday, my sister wore on Tuesday. We didn't care what anyone else thought. We were happy and content. We continued this pattern throughout elementary school.

My mom juggled two to three jobs at a time, so her schedule was hectic. You wouldn't know it by the way she balanced her time with us. She taught us early how to keep our bedrooms clean, our bodies washed, and our hearts pure. My mom also taught us to wear a positive attitude and a nice smile. The importance was not *what* you wear but *how* you wear it.

19 Eighty-Four

NO ORDINARY OPPORTUNITY – CLOG IT OR MOVE IT

"The thief comes only to steal and kill and destroy; I have come that they may have life, and have it to the full."

— [JOHN 10:10, NIV] —

This was the year I found out that golden opportunities aren't always in favor of the person desiring it.

My cousins and I always dreamed of owning a pair of clogs. They were these cute, wooden shoes with a buckle on top. I knew that if I didn't get a brand-new pair, I would eventually get them as hand-me-downs. I was ecstatic when my Aunt Mary purchased all the girls a pair in the summer. It didn't matter that they were extremely loud. They were fashionable. Some were open-toe, while others (like mine) were not. We couldn't wait until the next day to show them off at school. As soon as we walked into the building on the shiny, freshly buffed floor, the sound echoed throughout the entire school as we tried not to slip and break our necks. By the time we entered our separate classrooms, our teachers must've gotten the same idea to send us to the office. My teacher didn't even give me the chance to do what every elementary kid back in my day did when they wore a new pair of shoes— get up to sharpen my pencil. Even if you had a pencil that didn't need sharpening, you were awarded this chance for everyone to look down at your feet and see your new shoes. Who knew that clogs weren't included? I wanted to jump on the opportunity.

Eventually, we were all sent to the office to call home because our shoes were a distraction. The principal yelled, "TAKE THOSE LOUD SHOES OFF!"

NO ORDINARY WATCH DOG

Months later, my mom went outside to warm our car in the driveway before taking us to school. She did this every winter while she went back inside to finish preparing our lunch or helping me get on my snowsuit. It wasn't easy as a lefty. I looked like the little brother on *The Christmas Story*. Afterward, she would have us line up like soldiers and give us a dose of Cod Liver Oil. It tasted horrible, even when it was chased by a lemon drop. It may not have tasted good, but it was good for us because we never missed a day of school for being sick.

Too bad it didn't prevent thieves from stealing cars. The one who decided to steal our car sure knew not to wear clogs. He moved in silence. There was no automatic starter or auto locks while the car warmed in the driveway. So, my mom always had my sister looking out as the watchdog. "Watch the car, Katrina!" she would say. I guess it wasn't totally my sister's fault. Maybe my mom should've been more specific, like, "Keep an eye on the car to make sure no one runs off with it." My sister did exactly what my mom instructed. She *watched* the car as the thief got in, backed out of the driveway, and drove off with our car without mumbling a word.

"Where's the car, Katrina?" my mom asked in bewilderment.

"Gone!" my sister said softly as tears rolled down her face.

"What do you mean gone?" my mom interrogated.

"You said to watch it, Mama."

It was okay. God was watching. He made it so that the thief ran out of gas a few blocks from our home, leaving the car abandoned. The police notified my mom about where to pick it up. Isn't God amazing? Looking back, we could've been stranded on the way to school and my mom on her way to work.

NO ORDINARY TOUCH – HIDDEN SECRETS

God continued to keep His arms of protection around us, even when we didn't fully understand just who He was. But no one should ever feel like they need protection from the ones they love.

Although there was a lot of guilt, shame, and other things on my dad's end that caused his separation from my mom, we were too young to understand, plus my mother never talked negatively about our father to us. She let the spark shine in our eyes at the mention of his name, the sound of his voice when he would call, or the knock at the door when he would visit us during the summer.

The older we got, the dimmer the spark became. Over time, it faded. We were so desperate to reignite it that we ignored small things that weren't really small. We pretended things he did to us didn't actually happen because we wanted our dad.

Being with him, we learned how to try new things, whether it was games, food, or meeting new people. I remember trying this disgusting stuff in a jar called Pickled Herring. Other than that, I enjoyed the way he made breakfast. He would make the best scrambled eggs with onions and cheese you could wrap your taste buds around. Whether we had homemade or store-bought juice, he made a silly song and dance for us to do our parts in preparing the meal. We were the juice shakers. We would take turns grabbing the container of either apple, orange, cranberry, or grape juice and dance around the kitchen singing.

"Hold your hands out and close your eyes," he commanded, looking before we ate a meal. It didn't matter where we were; we had to place our hands in an upright position above the table while he quickly recited an Islamic prayer. I didn't know what he was saying. I just knew which word was the cue for digging in—"Amen!"

We had a lot of fun times. I loved playing "Mr. Snake" on long trips to amusement parks or visiting family and friends. He would drive with his knees while waving his hands to resemble a snake getting ready to attack. He periodically placed his left hand on the steering wheel while his right hand was on the prowl. My sister would usually sit in the back. She used to like playing the game when we were younger, but she acted like a party pooper the older we got.

"I'll play, Dad!" I said willingly. "Do me."

"Alright. Now remember Mr. Snake is hungry and likes to eat little girls," he would warn. "If you don't want him to eat you, don't move." He would start at my knee, squeezing tight while hitting every tickle spot. "Don't move," he stressed, moving higher and higher up my inner thigh. "Uh Oh! You moved! Mr. Snake has to eat you now!"

I guess I was too blind to see and hear a lot of subliminal messages. My sister did her best to protect me and keep my innocence. All the things our father did were camouflaged with fun stuff like playing arcade games or visiting state parks, amusement parks, zoos, or state fairs. I remember this time he took us fishing in the Pacific Ocean while visiting relatives in California. "Be careful, Ka'thank and Nuke," he told my sister and me. "It's slippery." We were heading back to our vehicle. As we ascended on an incline, we had to climb over large rocks covered with sea moss (more like slime). It was too late. My sister was the first to lose her footing as she slipped on a rock. She fell right into the ocean. I fell shortly after. I thought a sea monster was attacking me. It was just a bundle of seaweeds that took pleasure in grabbing hold of me. Granted, the water where we started to climb was not that deep. Our dad still came to the rescue!

When we returned to our lodging destination, he had us take off our wet clothes while he "checked" us over. My sister was first. She came out half-dressed with a look on her face I had never seen before. I asked her what was wrong, but she wouldn't talk to me. Being the younger sister, I

18

assumed she was being mean to me again. Why didn't she say something?

When it was my turn to get checked, she pulled me close to her as if to say, "NO!" She stared at me like she had seen a monster. Still, she didn't utter a word. She just knew the way he touched us was not appropriate.

19 Eighty-Five

NO ORDINARY REASON OR SEASON

"To everything, there is a season, and a time to every purpose under the heaven: a time to be born, and a time to die; a time to plant, and a time to pluck up that which is planted."

— [ECCLESIASTES 3:1-2] —

Winter is probably my favorite season. I love the snow, particularly because of how it makes the surroundings look more picturesque. However, most people don't like this season because temperatures are lower and days are much colder since the sun is not active. This was the case for us one Christmas.

I learned not to let things get to me but to find ways to overcome them, no matter the reason or season.

God had already spared our lives in a fire a few years back when we lived in an apartment. We didn't have much— just a few green velvet furniture pillows we used as dining room chairs in the day, a couch in the evening, and a bed at night. We were content without having a bunch of stuff because we had each other. My mom always made my sister and me feel like we had the world. She didn't know it then, but she was our world. She kept everything in motion.

Eventually, we moved into my childhood home. It was a lovely two-bedroom ranch-style brick home with an attached garage. I loved that house. Our neighbors also loved it. It was the go-to house on the block. Apparently, burglars loved the house too—especially on this cold, winter day before Christmas.

NO ORDINARY CHRISTMAS

My mom had finally saved enough money to give us a healthy Christmas full of things we had never had before—toys, a typewriter, clothes, an Atari game system, and more. I hate to admit this, but I had torn back tiny pieces of wrapping paper in the corner of some gifts to get a sneak peek of what I would receive.

Later that afternoon, we went to Kmart to do some last-minute shopping. When we returned, my mom noticed that the garage door and side door were wide open. We had gotten robbed… on Christmas Eve! Who could do such a thing? It had to be a reason why someone would take from a family who had little to nothing financially. And why do it during the holiday season?

Even though my heart sunk to the bottom of my stomach, my mom assured us everything would be alright.

She must've stayed up all night because we had more gifts wrapped under the tree by morning. They were no ordinary gifts. They were homemade presents she had stitched

21

with love. One gift was a long, pink velvet robe with pink buttons.

Traditionally, we went to my grandmother's house. After my mom shared the devastating news, I couldn't believe what happened next. My cousins liked our gifts of love more than their expensive items. It was a wake-up call that, no matter the reason, we wouldn't let things ruin our season. I wish I had remembered this motto a few months later.

NO ORDINARY SEASON – NEW REASON, DIFFERENT SEASON

"UGH! Something's wrong with Nuka!"

Yep. Something was definitely wrong with me. I was no ordinary girl. My eyes were swollen so big that it looked as though I had been in a fight with Mike Tyson, Bruce Lee, and Muhammad Ali all at the same time and lost terribly in the 1st round.

I had allergies. After being outside in the yard with my grandmother (something I enjoyed doing every day after school), my eyes started to itch. I did what any 10-year-old would do— rubbed my eyes. That was the worst possible thing to do.

"Stop rubbing them, Nuke," my grandma said as she directed me towards the house.

"But they burn!" My drama queen mojo had kicked in about this time. For some reason, I began to limp as though I couldn't walk. I staggered as though the heavy-weight champion had pulled me in for another round. This temporary numbness continued until my grandmother and I reached the house to call my mom.

"Bobbie Jean, Nuke must be allergic to something I planted," my grandmother said.

The Black-eyed Susies seemed so innocent at first glance. However, they were vicious. After admiring their beauty for a couple of seconds, they attacked me. Their pollen assaulted my nostrils while their stems ambushed my eyes. It wasn't long before I couldn't see. My mother was called to the rescue to take me to the pediatrician. I was given an instant shot of liquid Benadryl. I was back to normal in no time. My parting instructions were, "DO NOT RUB YOUR EYES!"

It was easier said than done, plus I had to stay inside during pollen season. *What child likes to stay inside while everyone else is outside?*

NO ORDINARY BREAK

I had nearly missed the entire summer because I had a break within the break. We usually took naps while my grandmother watched her soap operas. When we were older, she just made us go outside during that time. One day, while pretending we were some of the actors and actresses on the soap operas, I started running from (what I thought to be) insects attacking me. I found out later that it was only a dried dandelion whose seeds had dispersed. When my cousin shouted, "What's that?" I took off running. I tripped on a cement block and fell face forward onto a wooden picnic table. As a result, I cracked my nose and one of my two front teeth. I couldn't catch a break.

When things healed, we went to a park up the street not far from my aunt's house. Haskell Park was the place to be since all of us were competitive—always trying to see who could swing the highest or do the coolest trick moves on the slide. When it was my turn on the slide, I tried avoiding someone who hadn't quite moved out of the way yet. All of a sudden, CRACK! My wrist had snapped. I didn't cry at first. I knew it was painful, but I couldn't show the people at the park, let alone my cousins, that I was weak. It wasn't until my cousins screamed "EWWW" and pointed at my wrist bone that popped up that I let it all out. "AAAHH!!!" I screamed from the top of my lungs. My mouth looked as though I was auditioning for a part on *The Walking Dead*.

As soon as I saw my wrist, I took off running like a bolt of lightning. I have no idea why I ran. It didn't make the pain stop faster. By the time my cousins caught up to me, I had fallen limp. Like clockwork, my mom had just gotten off work and had pulled into the driveway at my Aunt Mary's house. My cousins practically carried me to the car. After my mom quickly gathered the 5-w's (who, what, when, where, and how), she raced me to the nearest hospital.

We were there for hours. We would've been discharged sooner, but my wrist wasn't set right after the first attempt to take me out of my misery. They had to rebreak it to set it again. Talk about pain! The doctor's parting words of encouragement since school was soon to start were, "At least you'll have a break from writing for about six weeks." Wrong! I was no ordinary student. I was left-handed. I had broken my right wrist. Bummer!

After weeks of discomfort, itching, scratching, and having limited summer options, I wanted a break. I needed to be outside. Since I couldn't ride my bike up and down the sidewalk like everyone else, I wanted to at least hang out on the patio. I could, but not during allergy season. Whenever allergy season neared an end, the dry season began. Unfortunately, that was the beginning of my constant nose bleeds.

19 Eighty-Seven

NO ORDINARY FLOW

"And a woman was there who had been subject to bleeding for twelve years, but no one could heal her."

[LUKE 8:43]

Unlike the woman in the Bible whose issue stopped after suffering 12 long years, my issues had just begun. This was the year I experienced a series of matters, back-to-back. Through it all, God helped me keep my head above water. Like the woman, I believe God was teaching me how to press my way and keep it moving.

"Why did you pass the bathroom to tell me that your nose is bleeding?" my mom questioned as blood dripped down my face. I really don't know why I passed the bathroom to inform her of my dilemma. It just seemed like the logical thing to do. I thought moms got a kick out of being their child's hero. I didn't just want my mom to be a good mom; I wanted her to win Mother of the Year.

"Oh, Jamillah," she grumbled. "Tilt your head back and hold your nose." She handed me some Kleenex and commanded, "Go to the bathroom and hold your head over the sink. I'll be right in."

That was music to my ears. I was old enough to do this on my own, for goodness's sake, but moms make things better. I think the real reason my mom continued to do it for me after my many failed attempts was because I was no ordinary tween. I would get blood everywhere, even in the impossible places—on the floor, the walls, the tub, the toilet, the mirror, my clothes, and even my hair. It would look like an NCIS crime scene.

"It won't stop, Mom!" I screamed as the blood continued to flow. By the time my mom walked in, my hand was scarlet, and my head was pounding. She did her usual routine, splashing cold water on my face while she filled the sink with water. I guess this was to cool me off to help the blood clot. Usually, this would work. After so long, the flow would slow down and eventually cease. Not this time. The blood continued until it started coming from both nostrils. I couldn't catch a break!

I tried to remain optimistic. After all, my blood type is "be positive."

"Katrina? Could you bring me a rag and some ice for Jamillah?" she asked my sister. "Her nose is bleeding again." Why did she have to call for my sister? My sister always reminded my mom I was too big for all this. Her accuracy was beside the point, but still.

The ice-cold compression, the rag on the back of my neck, and the gobs of Vaseline stuffed in my nose using Q-Tips did the trick. After days, weeks, and sometimes months of continuous nosebleeds, my mom sought the help of doctors. A specialist decided it would be best to close my leaky blood vessels using a device to numb the insides of my nostrils. It worked!

NO ORDINARY ISSUE – SAME YEAR, DIFFERENT ISSUE

My nosebleeds finally stopped, and my issue of blood began. "Hey, Mom! Guess what? Jamillah's done started her menstrual," my mom informed my grandmother on the phone.

Why all the fuss about a teenager bleeding? Nobody made a big deal about my nose bleeding. I hurt with cramps, and it brought on migraine headaches. Plus, I was forced to wear these uncomfortable things called "pads." My mom said they were for my protection. *Protection from what? Embarrassment?* Who needed social media? All you needed was that one family member who would do the spreading for you. For our family, it was my Uncle Ray. He told practically everyone he knew. So, if pads were for my protection, I needed one that was about six feet tall or one large enough for my next embarrassing moment.

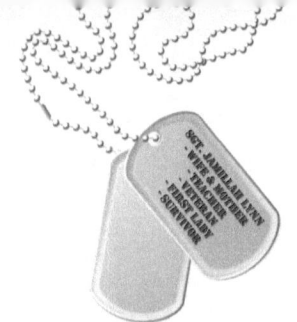

19 Eighty-Seven still

This was the year I learned how to face my fears. God was showing me then how He would never leave me alone to defeat any problem or giants in my life.

One day, a new word started circulating around Dort Elementary School. Those who knew were going around laughing and pointing at everyone they felt fit the description. After recess, they pointed in my direction. "Jamillah is a virgin!"

"No, I'm not!" I protested. I could've called on any of my so-called friends to defend my honor, but I called on my sister. "You can ask my sister. I ain't no virgin!"

"We don't need to ask your sister. She's one too." They may as well have talked about my mama. Now, they were itchin' for a scratch. "No, she's not! Don't ever call her or me that again, or I'll show you how not-of-a-virgin I am!" I threatened.

Boy, do I thank God I didn't have to show them what I promised. My sister came to the rescue. She confirmed what I was trying to tell them all along and dared anyone who thought differently. "Don't be calling my little sister a virgin. SHE AIN'T NO VIRGIN AND NEITHER AM I!" she protested. "You can ask our mama!"

Though we earned good grades and received several academic awards in elementary, we didn't quite know about street smarts and other stuff. Maybe we didn't know the word "virgin" at the time; we knew we had a thick bond.

NO ORDINARY SCHOOL – OLD SCHOOL VERSUS NEW SCHOOL

Civic Park was a new school for us. It had all the bells and whistles as any new school – fear, unfamiliarity, and embarrassment. Although my sister and I never had any problems finding new friends, we couldn't escape the label of being "good girls." We had to learn to stand our ground.

As we walked home from school one day, some boys walking on the opposite side of the street were trying to holler at my sister. Their flirtatious comments turned into rude, disrespectful insults when they realized she wasn't having it. She warned me just to ignore them, but when the words "YO MAMA" echoed from one of the boys' mouths, it was on!

"Don't talk about my mama, wit yo SCARY CURL-LOOKING-SELF!"

The boy's friends laughed so hard it made the guy angrier. When he began crossing the street towards us with balled fists and clenched teeth, it was my turn to have my sister's back. I got right behind her back and yelled, "GET 'EM, TRINA!"

Another day, while waiting my turn to jump rope during recess, I overheard some boys beatboxing and rapping. I got my sister's attention and laughed. Somehow, the guys must've gotten wind of my displeasure because the attention suddenly turned towards us. We were instantly challenged to a face-off.

It seemed as if the whole school gathered around to see us new girls attempt to put a stomping on the boys. My heart seemed to jump out of my chest. I couldn't back out now. It was my time to have her back.

My sister had the lyrics, and I had the beat. We rocked from side to side, hyping the crowd. We were like junior versions of Salt and Pepa. I balled my fist, puckered my lips, and pressed them in the crack between my thumb and pointer finger. By the time my fist left my face, and the lyrics stopped, everyone cheered in awe.

It was over. We no longer had to walk in fear.

19 Eighty-Eightish

NO ORDINARY CHURCH

"Let no one despise your youth..."

[1 TIMOTHY 4:12A]

This was the year God revealed Himself to me in my youth. It was no ordinary experience.

My aunt would pick my sister and me up for church on occasion. We wore our Sunday best, which consisted of a beautiful dress handmade by my mom. My mom usually washed and pressed our long, thick hair the night prior. The only thing left to do was put on our black patent leather shoes and white lace gloves. We were ready to attend Sunday School.

After learning about the Bible basics, the teachers would lead us to the fellowship hall to give us a snack. Didn't they realize that was the worst thing to do for young people? You can't feed us, make us sit still afterward for hours, and expect us not to fall asleep. It was torturous, to say the least. Still, I was grateful because it was my introduction to Christ.

A few years later, I developed a deeper understanding of who God was when my mom allowed my sister and me to visit a family friend's church on a youth night. She was very protective of us. She didn't allow us to spend the night at friends' houses or hang out after school. We couldn't give out our phone numbers, have boyfriends, or wear makeup at this age. She told us to enjoy our youth. So, I was shocked when my mom said, "YES," after asking if we could go.

I had to be sure she truly meant "yes" because it didn't turn out so well the last time she gave the okay for something.

"Don't ask me for nothin' when we're in the store! Don't be coming in and out of *my* house. And don't be outside after the streetlights come on."

In addition to these forbidden rules, we had to be in bed by 9:00 p.m. on any given school night. Staying up past that time only happened a few times a year: On Christmas and New Year's Eve, whenever the *Wizard of Oz* came on, and whenever Michael Jackson released a new video. Other than that, we had to BEAT IT!

One time, my cousins and I noticed how my mom had been in a good mood all day. She was giving us snacks, refills on Kool-Aid, and even letting us have company over. So, when everyone urged me to ask if we could continue to play outside in our skates moments before the streetlights, I thought, *"Why not?"*

"Hey, Mommy," I said while taking off my skates as she sat peacefully inside at the kitchen table sewing. "I was wondering if we could keep playing outside a little longer?"

"Sure!" she said quietly. It was a bit odd. But I overlooked the sarcasm in her voice, and my eyes lit up like a Christmas tree.

"Reeeaaally, Mom?" I said with enthusiasm.

"Go right ahead," she insisted as she waved the green light. "You can stay out as long as you like."

Oh boy, I couldn't get my skates on fast enough before returning outside to share the good news. It was a dream come true, more like a nightmare.

We were having way too much fun to notice that my mom had a switch in her hand. "Hi, Mom. You're the best!" I smiled and said.

"Is that so?" she replied sarcastically with a smirk on her face. Then, out of nowhere, her arms went to work on our legs using the switch. We looked like we were on one of those episodes of *Scooby Doo*. Our legs were moving, but we weren't going anywhere. Our neighbors were so afraid that they took off running.

That had been the last time I had asked her for permission to do something she told us *not* to do. So, I had my fingers crossed regarding church.

"Do you mean it, Mom? Can we really go to Youth Night?" I asked with amazement.

"Yes, Jamillah." She always called me by my real name when she was serious or irritated. "Just be back by 9:00. It's a school night!"

NO ORDINARY NIGHT - YOUTH NIGHT

When we arrived at this freshly painted white church with blue trimming, there were so many young people. I couldn't believe how packed it was on a school night. Some were in the back of the church doing homework. More were in the front, being attentive and involved.

Youth night was hype. My favorite part was playing Bible Drill. This segment was intense. You had to be mentally, physically, and spiritually prepared for this, or you could die – not literally, but your feelings could. It was imperative to know your books of the Bible, whether they were in the Old or New Testament, and the difference between their titles like St. John versus III John. Secondly, you had to be fast. When the caller said the scripture, you had to be the first to stand up and shout out the first two words of that verse once you found it in the Bible.

Talk about pressure. You were not only in competition with other young people, but adults as well who had years of experience. Some might say I was an EXTRA extrovert because I didn't mind jumping in and trying new things. I was no ordinary teenager.

When I first tried Bible Drill, I didn't even score a point. The young people that did score never placed 2nd or 3rd. And, unless you were the Bible Drill Queen (one of the missionaries there), you could forget about placing 1st. She would earn an average of 35 points compared to everyone's single digits. It inspired me to study the books of the Bible at home. When I returned the next week, I finally got my name on the board. The week after that, I scored even more points.

As time went on, I became more active in the church. Whenever my sister or I needed a ride to church, various ones would take turns picking us up for church and dropping us off at home, honoring my mother's request of having us home by 9:00 p.m. on a school night. We were known as "The Millah Girls," even though I was the youngest.

After months of going at Bible Drill, I finally beat one of the adults who usually placed 2nd. Week after week, I held the 2nd place title. Then, one night, I tied in 1st place with "The Queen." We were given another chance to break the tie. I blocked out the sounds of babies crying, the rustling of pages, or anyone trying to get my attention. Then, I waited for the part everyone looked forward to – the scorekeeper reading off the totals. She read several names, including "The Queen's." Finally, she exclaimed, "LET'S CONGRATULATE SISTER JAMILLAH AS OUR 1ST PLACE WINNER!"

It was a day of celebration not only for me but for every young person. It gave me hope that I could achieve my dreams and conquer my goals if I put my mind to it.

NO ORDINARY SUNDAY

One Sunday, the choir sang a powerful song. The words pierced my heart and soul. I felt warm inside. The feeling that came over me was indescribable. Before I knew it, tears were filling my eyes. The more I tried to hold them in by bulging my eyes, the stronger the feeling overpowered me. I didn't care. I couldn't hide it. I was experiencing my first touch from the Lord. It was no ordinary feeling.

19 Eighty-Eight still

NO ORDINARY SCHOOL - MONKEY IN THE MIDDLE

"Train up a child in the way he should go, and when he is old he will not depart from it."

[PROVERBS 22:6]

We played several games growing up – Dodge Ball, Kickball, Hopscotch, Hide-N-Seek, and Monkey in the Middle. I only liked playing Dodge Ball and Monkey in the Middle if I was one of the ones throwing the ball. Only people who were good at strategizing didn't mind being in the middle. For me, it was never fun, and that's how middle school started. I was grateful that God showed me how to focus more on the ball and not act like a monkey this year.

I was always letting my mouth get me in trouble. It followed me from elementary to middle school. In fact, most of my report card comments read, "Jamillah is smart and a pleasure to have in class." For days absent, it would be "zero." For citizenship comments, it would read, "Talks too much."

As a result, my teachers were constantly changing my seat. Between the teacher and the other students, who were the primary reason why I talked, I felt like the monkey in the middle. If it were a boy kicking my chair or pulling my hair, I would yell, "STOP IT!" I could've informed the teacher, but when I tried doing that before, the teacher would get annoyed at me or say, "Just learn how to ignore it." *Ignore it? How could I when these things continually happen?*

I got tired of staying in for recess for my constant blurt-outs, and my mom grew tired of being called to the school. She would have to leave work or be awakened from sleep between jobs.

One day, the teacher announced we had a new student. I couldn't believe it was the same boy who teased me in elementary school. To make matters worst, he sat right behind me. He wasted no time irritating me at the start of class. I don't know why the teacher never heard or saw what he was doing to me, but I felt my temperature rising. I can't remember if he started by throwing spitballs in my hair, pieces of his eraser at me, or by calling me Olive Oyl – a skinny cartoon character on *Popeye*. I wanted to punch him. Instead, I remembered my mom's last discussion with me after being called at work regarding my mouth, "Jamillah, I'm so sick of hearing about Charles. He's probably picking on you because he likes you. That's what boys do. I tell you what, though, this is the *last* time I better be called to come up here! You hear me?"

I nodded my head, "*Yes!*" I was under duress. She had me by the collar and pinned up on a wall. She gritted her teeth and used her skinny lip approach. To top it off, she made her eyes bulge at me. They seemed like they would pop out and shoot me in the face. I *had* to agree, or else I could've lost my life. Instead of yelling, "Leave me alone," I gave him a mean look and continued doing my class-work. Then, my pencil lead broke. I took a deep breath and counted to ten before getting up to sharpen it because I knew he might do something to irritate me. Surprisingly, he didn't bother me on the way to sharpen my pencil. He decided to trip me on my way back to my seat.

That was the last straw. I turned into the female version of the Hulk, picked up my chair, and threw it at him. The fight between Charles and I began. After we were broken up, my teacher pointed to the door without hesitation or saying a word. I knew what it meant – to the principal's office.

NO ORDINARY LECTURE

While waiting in the principal's office, it seemed as if all my other teachers had business to attend that day. By the look on my face, they knew I was in trouble. I was able to keep my composure and keep a straight face until my English teacher entered the room. She didn't know it, but she was my favorite teacher. The only downside to it was that she was friends with the principal. I felt they would tag team my punishment.

"Miss McClendon, why are you in here?"

"I…"

"I know you are not about to tell me that you got your-self in trouble with this here young man, are you?"

"I…"

"Because if you are, I am going to be sadly disappointed. You're supposed to be smart, and smart people make smart

choices. I don't know this young man, but I do know you...
or, at least I *thought* I knew you. Are you, in fact, smart?

At this point, I knew I wouldn't be able to get a word in
edge-wise. I didn't know whether to answer or wait for Mrs.
Speights to respond to her own question.

"Miss McClendon? Answer me, please. Are you
smart or not?"

I played it safe and nodded my head. Tears began to
fill my eyes, and I couldn't fight them back any longer. She
continued to tell me how happy she was to have me in her
class. She went on to say how she believed in me and depended on me to be one of the ones to help make the world
a better place to live in. She reminded me that I could do it
if I made better choices for myself.

By the time she finished her lecture, the principal had
come out of his office. Instead of calling Charles or me to
enter, he spoke with Mrs. Speights. Apparently, she talked to
him and made a compromise that I would work my punishment off with her. She would talk to me and discuss other
ways I could channel my frustration and focus my attention
on my education.

When my punishment period ended, it was the start of a
new and improved Jamillah. I began paying more attention
in class, improved my citizenship, and stopped blaming
others for my decisions. From this, I was selected to receive
the Principal's Award two years in a row, an award given
in middle school to a student that has shown growth in
academics, behavior, character, and attitude. That person
was me. I no longer played "the monkey" when it came to
my education.

19 Eighty-Nine

NO ORDINARY FRESHMAN – HI SCHOOL

*"But as for you, continue in what you have
learned and have firmly believed..."*

— [2 TIMOTHY 3:14A] —

This was the year God prepared me to venture out and embrace new surroundings, friendships, and opportunities.

As excited as I was to attend the same school as my sister, I was not mentally ready to leave middle school and say "hello" to high school. I would no longer see my middle school friend, middle school crush, or neighborhood pals. They all chose to go to my soon-to-be rival school.

I felt comfort in knowing I would at least be with my sister. I figured I could see her in the hallways between classes, sit by her at lunch, or spend time with her after school. Instead, she had already established her friendships and the people with whom she hung with. Her classes were in a different part of the building. She was also in the marching band. To me, that was a girl's equivalent to being in sports. This meant I had no chance of hanging with my 13-year running bestie.

I was no ordinary freshman. I didn't like the same things most people my age liked. I liked boys, but I didn't care about having a boyfriend. I liked dressing up and dressing nice, but I didn't worry about wearing the latest clothing fashions. My main concerns were going to school and getting my education. Sure, I developed friendships and helped others along the way, but if it didn't concern academic achievement, I didn't want any part of it.

To get through this new life, I kept myself busy. I joined Science Olympiad, a club where students studied various scientific areas to help prepare for competitions. I really enjoyed it, but it required more time than I could put in. It was the same for the marching band. That's why I chose to join the concert band.

Unlike everyone else, I dressed up every day and wore pumps to school. When I chose to wear nothing but skirts, suits, or dresses, my mom supported my decision. Knowing we didn't have the money to splurge on a new wardrobe, she converted all my pants to skirts. People were fascinated by seeing the first Levi denim and colored skirts. I also styled my hair differently every day. I had to. This was the year my sister said, "I'm done doing your hair. If you want it a certain way, learn how to do it yourself." I couldn't believe it. How could she abandon me like this and leave me with such a massive task? Granted, I was slightly irritating when it came to parting my hair. If it were off by a strand or if a braid was too tight or tighter than the other, I would plead and beg for her to redo it. She would threaten that it was her last time, but she never stuck to it until I became a freshman. I guess if I weren't myself, I would be tired of me also.

Her refusals helped push me to do it myself and eventually prepared me to become a fairly good hairstylist. I learned how to do the latest styles like the French Roll and bun. I created what my sister called "the Egyptian Part." It was inspired by my Aunt Mary's Zig Zag Part or "Egg Crack." People would be amazed to learn that I did my own hair, especially when I figured out how to braid my hair upwards.

Aside from doing my homework and earning good marks on my report card, I focused on saving money, how I dressed, and how I styled my hair. In fact, I used to keep a log of what I wore each day to school and church in a journal that my mom gave me so as not to repeat the same outfit twice in the same month. After school, I would log how much money I had in my money factory machine. It was a black machine with clear slots that sorted each coin. I saved so much money that I had to put the overflow in my pink piggy bank my mother made for me in a ceramics class. I had money for lunch and other school-related events. This was probably one of the reasons why math was my favorite subject and why I loved numbers so much.

19 Ninety-Three

This was one of my most challenging years so far. After another inappropriate encounter with my father, my sister made me inform our mom. When my mom confronted him, he told her I was dreaming and had made it all up. Even after failed attempts of writing him letters to get him to admit and move forward, it caused a wedge between us. On top of it, my mom was involved in a situation at her job that resulted in her spending extensive time away from home. My sister was married with her first child, so her time was devoted to being a young wife and mother. My support team and comfort circle were practically gone.

Like film placed in a dark room, this was the year God helped develop me.

I waited for so long to become a senior, mainly because all the other girls in my graduation class had developed into their adult bodies. In my opinion, they had the looks, the ideal body shape, the latest fashions in clothing and shoes, and the hottest rides in the student parking lot. I was still praying and asking my mom when I would graduate from a training bra. I can still hear my Aunt Gloria reminding me that everyone develops at different stages. She also said, "Don't rush. Wait on your time. When that time comes, you'll wish you hadn't asked."

"Girl, do you know you have the highest GPA in our class? I didn't know you were that smart," one of the girls in my senior class asked me while preparing to write an ad in the school's newspaper. For four years, I didn't focus on being the top student; I only focused on doing my best. Apparently, my best pushed me to the top of my class with over 215 seniors.

Before I knew it, I was getting praised for being the Valedictorian. I got called down to the principal's office to take a photo.

"Jamillah, do you know why you are here?"

"Yes, to take a photo."

"That, and to let you know your hard work has paid off. Your achievements have earned you a spot on television's 'Best of the Class!' Congratulations!"

NO ORDINARY NOMINATION

I couldn't wait to share the news of my academic achievements with my mom and sister. Teachers congratulated me in the hallway all day for holding such a wonderful title. I shook hands with people I didn't even know as I walked to each of my classes. In the following days, I was called to the office to take pictures for various titles in the school paper. I was nominated and named *Most Ambitious*, *Best Hair*, *Most Likely to Succeed*, and *Best Dressed*. I couldn't believe it. Though everyone's main suspense was to see who was voted best couple or had the best car, it was nice. After all, the school newspaper was something all students couldn't wait to read.

NO ORDINARY DEPARTURE

Twelve years of going to school were finally coming to an end. I had to prepare myself mentally for my future. I was tempted to participate in National Skip Day, but I didn't want to ruin my perfect attendance record. I also didn't want to let down people who were counting on me to make good choices. I was one of few seniors in school that day. I was allowed to go around filling up my senior book with signatures and words to remember from teachers and fellow classmates.

Before graduation, I was asked to give a speech at our school's honor assembly. I stayed up the night before to finalize it. When I arrived, everyone was confused as to why the class president didn't give the speech so that I could have words on graduation day. It didn't bother me. I was simply happy to share encouragement. When the night was over, the only thing left to prepare for was graduation day.

My best friend, Tanisha, helped me set up a hair appointment with her mom for graduation. My mother and sister wondered why I didn't style my own hair. I wanted the feel of getting it professionally done. It was styled in an upward four-inch crimped French Roll. Towards the front, there was a split in the middle where she glued in a zipper to appear as if my hair was unzipped. To maintain the look, it was stuck in place with hair spritz. Man, oh, man! You couldn't tell me nothing. When I arrived home later that night, my mom and sister couldn't believe I had chosen that particular hairstyle. I assumed they didn't like it, but I was wrong. They loved it. Their question was, "How in the world is *that* going to fit under your graduation cap?" I had no clue. Thinking about it made me sick.

On graduation day, I ironed my gown, put on a purple and white dress suit with heels, and met up at the Whiting Auditorium. I had my gold cords around my neck and lined up with the rest of the graduating class. I placed my cap on top of my mountain of a hairstyle, secured it with two bobby pins on either side and walked with pride as I waited anxiously for my name to be called.

It seemed like forever getting through all the letters of the alphabet before the "M's" were called. Then, it was time for my section to stand up to form a line at the bottom of the stage right steps. Behind the curtains, tears filled my eyes. It wasn't that I was nervous, especially regarding the mispronunciation of my name, because we were asked to write the sounding of our names on an index card. I wrote

"Juh-mill-uh." I was just happy for each individual before me as if it were me. I guess they were me. We were all in this together. So, when the announcer called my name, I put the largest smile on my face the world had ever seen. I waved at the crowd as if they knew me. I didn't know where my family was, but I knew they were somewhere out there being proud of me.

At the end of the ceremony, I moved my tassel from the right to the left and shouted with joy as we cheered, "Class of 1993!" It was time to say "goodbye."

19 *Ninety-Four*

NO ORDINARY CALL

"Nevertheless, each person should live as a believer in whatever situation the Lord has assigned to them, just as God has called them..."

[1 CORINTHIANS 7:17]

I spent so much time doing what I felt others wanted me to do instead of what God desired for me. Before I wasted more time going in the wrong direction, He gave me a hard knock on the head. This was the year I was shown how to properly answer my calling.

Being at the top of my class was one thing. Remaining at the top required discipline and structure. I lacked those qualities at the time, not because I didn't want to, but because I never had to exercise them. Everything I achieved had come easy. Obtaining an academic scholarship and being awarded a few grants was a blessing.

I chose to attend the University of Michigan. For one, it was close to home. Secondly, it was where my sister attended.

After taking the placement tests, I scored high and was placed into advanced-level classes. I didn't know I could register for the lower-level classes, ace them, and work my way up. Instead, every class I placed in, I registered for. My full-time freshman schedule consisted of Calculus II, Biology, Art, and English Literature. Ironically, I aced Calc and English Lit, held a C in Art, and was gradually failing biology.

I imagined college life to be similar to high school. WRONG! I used to study the night prior, take a few minutes going over my notes, and ace the test the next day. Now, it required reading, re-reading, asking questions, and study groups – all of which I chose to ignore. Art required studying the genres, styles of painting, and various artists. It meant thinking about the mood and emotions behind the paintings or drawings. Basically, it required more work than I was willing to put in.

I was too embarrassed to ask for help. I assumed everyone would be disappointed that I, "Miss Four-Point-'O'," was indeed struggling in her first year in college. So, I kept it to myself. I didn't even talk to my counselor, who could have provided me with more options. Instead, I kept going to class, getting deeper and deeper into a hole I couldn't dig myself out of. Even when I received a letter warning me that I was on the verge of losing my scholarship, I took the option of retaking the class.

I received my very first "D." I couldn't believe it. The "D" might as well have stood for "death" because I wanted to find the nearest rock, crawl underneath it, and die.

Not long after arriving home that day, I heard the phone ring. I thought to myself, *"I can't take any more bad news."* The voice on the other end sounded pleasant.

"Hello! Do you need money for college?"

"Yes, I do," I said without hesitation, thinking to myself, "*Perfect timing.*"

"Well, great. My name is Sergeant Sunday. I'm a recruiter for the United States Army Reserves. Would you like to hear more about earning money for college?"

"Sure."

I had done many internships in high school, attending colleges such as the University of Michigan – Ann Arbor and Michigan State University, where I was paid to solve various math and science probabilities. I also worked for companies such as Warner Lamberts, earning about $20 an hour. The job I had was creepy but adventurous. For every experience, my room and board were paid. I figured, "*How could this opportunity be any different?*"

"Great! I'll set up a meeting with you and your parents to discuss the details. How about tomorrow evening?"

When my mom came home, I told her about my conversation with the woman.

"Sergeant who?" my mom inquired with an angry look on her face. "I don't think so. She may be trying to trick you into joining the Army or something. I don't like the sounds of it."

"Mom. Trust me. It's not the Army. I'll be working *for* the Army and earning money for college. Basically, it's like another internship."

"Okay. Well, I'll see what this Sergeant Sunday is talking about."

The next day, we met with the recruiter. My mom asked a plethora of questions, and Sergeant Sunday gave my mother the answers she wanted to hear. It didn't matter to the recruiter that the responses were misleading. She was doing her job. Before she left, my mom asked her one more time, "Are you sure this isn't the Army and all that boot camp stuff?"

Sergeant Sunday raised her hand as if to swear and said, "You have my word."

It wasn't long before I received a packet in the mail with all the necessary information, including the date, time, location, and basic items needed. My mom and I went on a shopping spree. She bought me a Walkman, perfume sets, underwear, and more. Then, she glanced at the information packet and yelled, "Fort Lauderdale! That's in Florida. Ooh, Jamillah, you're going to love it there." She worked for AAA Travel Company for years, so I had no doubt she knew what she was talking about. To our surprise, the Fort Lauderdale she thought she saw was actually Fort Leonard Wood... MISSOURI!

NO ORDINARY TEST

Before making it to Missouri, I had to stop at an intake location in Detroit. I guess this was where a person was checked over to ensure they were physically, educationally, and mentally fit.

The physical exam included my eyes and ears. My vision was 20-20, and my hearing was great. The staff was concerned about my weight. I was a buck o five soaking wet. Given my age, gender, and height, I needed to be at least 110 to 115 pounds to proceed, but I was given a pass and encouraged to gain weight or muscle.

The last part of the physical was physical. I was touched from head to toe. I had to lay down on my back and spread my legs. After checking my "internal temperature," the doctor looked at the nurse taking notes and said, "Hymen intact." I had no idea what that meant. When they were done asking me to touch my toes, bend at my waist, and walk back and forth, I was able to get dressed.

The next day, I had to take a test called the ASVAB (Armed Service Vocational Aptitude Battery). It was an assessment to help the military determine whether I was a good fit to join the service. Additionally, it showed which branch of service might be best for me. The better my ASVAB score, the broader my options.

At the end of the day, I waited in a long line to review my scores with decorated personnel and choose a job title called a M.O.S. (Military Occupational Service code). The serviceman's face showed that I scored pretty high on my ASVAB test. He said, "You can go into the medical field!" Without hesitation, I said, "Sure!"

NO ORDINARY DAY

Each day, a group of us left the intake location to return to our hotel rooms. My roommates and I quickly became friends over the course of three days. I assumed we were all heading to the same final destination, but it depended on our jobs, duty stations, and where we were assigned. I was sent to Misery (Mi-ssour-i). It was time for me to toughen up and fast.

19 *Ninety-Four still*

A president doesn't jump into the role of a president. He begins as a senator or a governor. A doctor starts as an intern. A lawyer is first a paralegal, and a teacher starts as a student. Everyone has to start somewhere. Mine was in boot camp. This was the year God prepared me to be a soldier by starting as a private.

"Where am I," I thought to myself. I was dressed for what I assumed to be an interview or an internship. I had on a two-piece suit with black two-inch heels. My hair was freshly permed and in a fancy updo.

"So, what do we have here?" the drill sergeant bellowed as he pointed me out. "Maybe she thinks she's going to the *Miss Ebony Fashion Show*."

"I'm not supposed to be here," I cried!

He and the other drill sergeants must've assumed I was joking because they turned to each other and laughed even harder. One said, "Private, look around 'cause for the next couple of months, ten weeks to be exact, this will be your new home. Now move it, gather your things and step in line!"

As if things couldn't get any worse, it began to rain. Like a deer in a headlight, I couldn't move. It's not like I didn't care about getting wet; I was just in a state of shock. After a while, a young man feeling sorry for me gathered my luggage and started carrying them to our destination. No sooner than I could smile and thank him, one of the drill sergeants yelled something like, "Soldier, either you drop her bags, or you drop!" He chose the first option. I couldn't help but think to myself, *"He was only trying to be polite. Where are the gentlemen?"* I soon realized that we were no longer men or women; we were soldiers. We weren't ladies or gentlemen; we were privates, and they were drill sergeants.

I wasn't equipped for this kind of trip. Who in their right mind would hike a mile in the rain… up a hill… in heels? "Let's go, Soldier," I heard echoing in my ears. In an instant, I kicked on my autopilot switch and started to move. With each step, I felt like I was getting further behind. The distance seemed to disappear instead of getting closer. But just when I thought I couldn't bear to take another step, we arrived. It was a large, brown building that smelled like the inside of an old storage unit; only it was much hotter. Although we arrived in the late evening, it was super loud and extra bright. There were sergeants everywhere shouting, "Let's go, Soldier! Empty your bags!"

"Empty my bags?" I said to myself. It took me all day to pack everything nice and neat. Why would I want to empty everything, especially in front of all these strangers—correction soldiers? Who did he think he was anyway? He had no right. Still, I found myself in the same boat as all the others—dumping our things, even our personal items, on long tables displayed for all the world to see. I had to practically dump everything I had in the "GET-RID-OF-IT-BIN" because they weren't allowed. The straw that broke the camel's back was when I had to get rid of all the perfume sets I had saved up to buy.

To my far left was a line with a man holding a razor and another man holding up scissors. The men had to get their hair shaven in what they called a crew cut. The women had a choice to either get their hair shaven or cut. Anyone who knew me could imagine me fainting at this point. My hair was halfway down my back and thick too. Someone in front of me whispered, "You don't have to get yours cut if you keep your hair pinned up above your collar." I felt relieved.

To my immediate left, we were given a large, green duffle bag in which we were to place our remaining personal and Army-issued items. We were given physical training (PT) uniforms, battle dress uniforms (BDUs), uncomfortable black boots, and a few things we would need in the weeks ahead.

To my right, several soldiers were collecting linen for their bunks. Everything was the same size and color. I scurried over to the line and received my pile: a pillow, two flat sheets, and a cover. There was no such thing as a fitted sheet. The pillow was striped (white and blue) with feathers sticking out every time it was squeezed. The sheets were white and felt like a starched paper towel. The wool blanket was super itchy and uncooperative, especially when it was time to make our beds.

"Lights out!" one of the drill sergeants screamed. I thought to myself, *"Wow, he didn't even give me a chance to shower, brush my teeth or say my prayers."* It was the first night I said my prayers in my bed instead of on my knees. That entire night was a blur to me. I wanted badly to call home. I hadn't spoken to my mom since I had left Michigan days ago.

NO ORDINARY TRUCK

At 0530 hours (5:30 a.m.), we were awakened by the loud voice of a drill sergeant yelling, "LET'S GO, PRIVATES! MOVE IT!" I thought to myself, *"He needs a chill pill… and fast."* We had minutes to use the restroom, brush our teeth, make our beds, retrieve our items, and line up in front of the bus. It was called a cattle truck, mainly because it was identical to the type of vehicle cows were hauled in. There were no seats, only windows.

"Hurry up and move," the irritated drill sergeant yelled out again. We had to place our Army-issued green duffle bags in front of us and pile in (face forward) behind the person ahead of us. In my opinion, the truck's capacity was about 50 people without luggage. They seemed to squeeze 100 of us in there with luggage.

"Push, Privates. Stop your whining and move forward!"

"Move forward? There's not even enough room to breathe."

We seemed to have traveled in this standing position for hours. It was probably 15 to 20 minutes, but not knowing why or where we were going altered my sense of time. Being crammed like a pack of sardines altered my sense of smell.

"Everybody out! Move it! Let's go. You privates are moving like pond water. GET OUT!" I had no idea why all the drill sergeants yelled. It's like they all carried chips on their shoulders. It made me want to hug them and say, "Jesus loves you." However, I felt it would make them yell even more. One of them had already sprayed spittle on my face. It was disgusting. I probably would've vomited if it had landed on my lip.

"You, right here. Faster," one of the drill sergeants yelled.

Another one said, "Let's go, Soldier! Empty your bags," as he pointed to the ground. This was the second time I had to dump all my things out. They called it a shakedown. Maybe they wanted to be extra sure that we had nothing personal entering boot camp. Either way, I seemed to be the last one trying to place my things nice and neatly in my duffle bag. If I didn't want the rest of my items confiscated, I had to throw them in the bag quickly. Afterward, I did. I was ordered to follow a group in one of the buildings. Inside these brown, brick three-story buildings called "barracks" were rooms we would call home for the next nine weeks.

NO ORDINARY BUDDY

I was assigned a battle buddy (partner). By the time I entered our room, she had already chosen her bed and had her things unpacked and in her wall locker. I was too afraid to ask questions and too embarrassed to introduce myself. I didn't want to come off as crazy, so I bottled everything inside. I wanted to scream and yell, *"There's been a mistake!"* But there was no time for that, not even shedding a tear.

NO ORDINARY GRUB

After making my bunk and placing my items in my wall locker, we had to line up in formation and march to the chow hall. This was the Army's version of a cafeteria. We hadn't eaten anything since the night before, so we were all starving. The line was wrapped around the building. Our platoon of four squads seemed to be last on the list. The good news was that it stopped raining. As the line shortened, my stomach grew larger. I smelled the food from outside.

Inside, I looked around and saw nothing but soldiers eating like they hadn't eaten for days. They were like robots. They didn't talk, smile, or look up. They only ate as fast as they could. One guy guzzled down two cups of water like he was a fish. I must have been staring too hard. Suddenly, a drill sergeant saw me and said, "Eyes front, Private."

"Last four."

"Last four," looking puzzled?

"Last four, Private. What are your last four?"

"I don't know. My last four what?"

"Private, I ask the questions here. When I ask for your last four, you are to tell me the last four digits of your social security number!"

How in the world was I supposed to know that? I never needed to know my social security number, so I definitely didn't memorize it. Apparently, to eat, I had to give it to them.

"Who is this private's drill sergeant?"

"That'd be me," Drill Sergeant Mack acknowledged.

"This private needs her last four. Seems she doesn't know. So, I'm guessing she doesn't want to eat."

Sergeant Mack looked at me and asked, "You wanna eat, Private?"

"Yes, Sir," I yelled since everyone else was yelling. I thought that was the key. Unfortunately, it was to the wrong door. I must've said something wrong because all the noise seemed to stop.

"DID YOU JUST CALL ME 'SIR'? I WORK FOR A LIVING! YOU CALL ME 'DRILL SERGEANT'!"

"Yes, Sirr…. geant." I had to dress it up fast.

After my drill sergeant gave me my last four, I memorized them and repeated them over in my head. When I was asked again, I yelled it to the top of my lungs.

I couldn't wait to receive my tray and meal. Looking around, I realized that no one smiled or talked. We only had time to eat. Then, after we ate, we were required to drink two glasses of water. Even though there were various drink selections (including pop and juice), they were off limits to the new recruits.

NO ORDINARY DISCUSSION

Next, we marched to a huge building that looked like a warehouse. We were commanded to sit with our legs crisscrossed as we listened to different drill sergeants lecturing us on the rules of the base. Everything went in one ear and out the other since I didn't want to be there. I only wanted to know three things – when I could call home, what time we would eat next, and where to find the nearest restroom. They must've read my mind because all three questions were answered shortly after.

"The latrines are located in the rear. For those of you who have to pay your water bill, stand up and form a line. All you cry babies waiting to call home to your mamas, you will have time to do so after our last session. Chow time is in an hour."

I stood up and fell in the correct line to relieve myself. Just as the line shortened, another issue arose – my menstrual began! I couldn't believe it. I guess with all the emotions and adrenaline pumping, I jumpstarted my schedule. It couldn't have come at a worse time. Who could I tell? Who would allow me a chance to get cleaned up? On top of it all, I hadn't thought about packing protection. I assumed I would be at a resort, basking in the sun near a local shopping center. Instead, I was stuck… in a military prison called "Boot Camp."

When a stall was open, I sprinted in and relieved myself. To assist in my dilemma, I stuffed a wad of toilet paper in my underwear and prayed it would hold until our next "latrine break." I planned on restuffing toilet paper until someone asked or mentioned if there was a nearby store.

NO ORDINARY MESSAGE

I looked forward to the moment when they dismissed us. The magic words were "FALL OUT!"

We had a choice to go to the barracks and shower before lights out or wait in several long lines to call home. I needed to do both, but I chose the latter. I knew I wouldn't survive another day if I didn't. It was imperative that I share what was going on with someone who loved me.

There were about five pay phones. The lines extended for days, and we were only given two minutes each. How was I going to call home? I had no money and no phone card. I would've been able to do like everyone else around me and call collect, but I remembered my mom didn't accept collect calls. I was hoping and praying she would make an exception this time.

There were still ten soldiers ahead of me when one of the drill sergeants yelled, "Fifteen minutes!" Fifteen minutes? That left no time for me if everyone could talk their two minutes. I needed my chance to call. I began to pray and ask God to grant me favor. I asked Him to do the impossible and let time stand still.

When it was my turn, I heard another drill sergeant say, "Time to wrap it up!" I panicked and ran to the pay phone the very second the soldier in front of me hung it up. It was hot and sweaty. I didn't want to put the top part anywhere near my ear. The bottom part smelled like a porter potty. I didn't care. I quickly wiped it off and proceeded.

My heart nearly jumped out of my chest as I turned the dial to zero.

"Hello. This is the operator. How may I place your call?" I gave her the phone number with the area code included. "Please state your name."

"Mama! I'm in the Army. Help!"

The operator called my mom and said, "You have a collect call from 'Mama-I'm-In-The-Army-Help.'" Before my mom could accept or decline the charges, I had to hang up.

"Let's go, privates," the drill sergeant demanded.

NO ORDINARY SHOWER

I was one of about forty women fighting for a shower when the female drill sergeant came in and yelled, "Hurry it up! You have 15 minutes before lights out, and you don't want to find out what happens if you're not in your bunks!" I spent half of that time in the restroom stall.

I knew I couldn't survive another day stuffing my underwear with toilet paper for protection. I spotted a sanitary napkin dispenser, but it required a dime. It did me no good. When I asked if anyone had any sanitary napkins, they ignored me. They were busy trying to jump in the shower. It was an eight-by-eight-foot open area with no doors. With four shower heads on each side, girls were tripled up on each shower head, rinsing off soap or shampoo out of their hair. I couldn't do anything but stare in shock.

"Girl, you better hurry up. That drill sergeant ain't no joke," one of the girls told me.

I joined two other females under a shower head and did the fastest version of a shower I could do. There was no more hot water, so the cold water helped rush me along.

"FIVE MINUTES," the female drill sergeant yelled.

I still hadn't dried off, put on lotion or deodorant, or my sleeping uniform, which was also used for PT. I did my best, along with about ten other female soldiers who were left. We scrambled around, trying to put our things back in our shower bags without slipping and falling. Mostly everyone made it back to their rooms in time except four other girls and me. We were told to meet outside in a formation. We had to march to an open field where we were lectured and disciplined about the importance of time.

NO ORDINARY DRILL

The drill sergeants took turns making us pay. We had to extend our arms at shoulder height on either side and rotate them in a circular motion forward and backward. If we lowered them, we had to do push-ups. It annoyed them that I kept wiping my hands off every time I got back up. So, I had to drop and give them more. When my arms could take no more, I refused to perform another command.

"Is there a problem, Private?" Drill Sergeant Russell asked.

When I didn't reply, he looked at Drill Sergeant Johnson and said, "Looks like we got us a tough one." She nodded in agreement and dismissed the other females to finish their punishment by cleaning the restroom.

"Are you tough, Private?" he asked, getting in my face.

I felt my emotions getting the best of me. It was already the wrong time of the month. I didn't want to answer "Yes" because crying made me contradict myself. If I had responded with a "No," I would've given them the upper hand. So, I refused to answer.

"Private, I suggest you answer my question if you want to get out of here. I know your type. You think you're all tough, but inside you're weak. I bet you still wet your pants, don't you? I bet you still cry home like a little baby and wait for your mama to feed you a warm bottle of milk."

Why did he have to mention my mama? "I WANT TO GO HOOOOOOOOME!" By this time, it had started raining again.

"You want to go home, huh?" Drill Sergeant Johnson asked. "Well, I suggest you start by following orders. The faster you do that, the faster we'll send you home to your mama. Now roll right."

I rolled right down a hill. I rolled left up the hill. I got motivated, thinking I would get my papers to go home.

NO ORDINARY NIGHT

Someone placed a few sanitary napkins on my bunk. After putting them away, I went to sleep, hoping to go home soon. The next day was our physical fitness test. How could I take a test when I was still in a state of shock?

"Sound off!" one of the drill sergeants said at 0530 hours. "You're ONE (pointing to someone in front of me)." I was TWO, and the persons behind me continued the count all the way to about EIGHT.

"All ONE's in this line. TWO's in this line. THREE's line up here and so forth." Everything was done in formation: going to the restroom, the chow hall, getting uniforms. You name it. Now, I had to line up to make a fool out of myself in front of complete strangers.

The first of three tests was doing pushups. We had two minutes to do as many as we could. I had never done one before in my life. I could blame my high school gym teacher (I forgot his name), who only taught us the fundamentals of basketball, the basics of swimming (in which I nearly drowned), jump rope, and relay racing. I guess I should give him credit for showing us how to climb a rope, but what good was that going to do me at this point? My arms were as useful to me as toothpicks are for canoeing – worthless! There was no such thing as "girl pushups." Everyone was given the same instructions. The pushup was not counted

65

if you didn't go high enough to make a 180-degree line or down low enough to make a 90-degree angle. Once you fell to your knees, the count was over. Therefore, after several attempts of squirming, grunting, and grinding my teeth, I could only do five. My arms were sore from last's night sample drills. For my age, height, gender, and weight, I was supposed to do a minimum of about 15.

The next category was sit-ups. After a partner had held my feet, my two-minute time clock started. Unlike pushups, I managed to knock them out of the park. The minimum requirement was about 50, and the maximum was 80. I exceeded by doing 108. That was almost one sit-up a second. People looked at me like I had some type of superpower. I needed this moment, even though it was just a moment. I needed something to motivate me for the final event – the two-mile run.

NO ORDINARY RUN

I was a fairly good sprinter in track. The only running I had ever done outside of that was a quick dash to the house or car whenever I got caught in the rain. This military-run was something different.

"You are being tested on your ability to complete a two-mile course in the shortest time possible. Although walking is authorized, it is strongly discouraged…" the announcer called out. "Any questions?"

"Yeah. Can I go home, please?" I said to myself.

We had to line up across a long open road. It was one mile down and one mile back. I started like Peter Rabbit. I had slowed down to a snail's pace by the halfway mark.

I looked off to the side for people to pass out Gatorade or water as I did back home as a volunteer during the Crim Festival of Races. No one called cadence or called out my name to cheer me on. It was just the Lord and me with the heavy sounds of deep breathing and tons of dripping sweat – the salty kind that burns your eyes and makes your face sticky.

Eventually, I stopped running and began to walk. That was probably the worst thing I could have done. It caused me to feel every ache, pain, cramp, and weight of my body all at once.

"Nineteen minutes thirty seconds," I heard the announcer call as I approached.

He continued counting through the sounds of those who had already finished the run. It was enough to give me my second wind. That's when I gave it all I had. I crossed the finish line at 20 minutes and some change. I saw my Drill Sergeant and said, "Mac…". I was too tired to say my full last name, McClendon.

"Private Mack. Gotcha," my drill sergeant recorded.

My run time didn't meet the requirements. When it was over, I walked it off and caught my breath. Finally, we marched to the chow hall for breakfast, and I had a moment of hope.

19 *Ninety-Five*

NO ORDINARY TRAINING

"Therefore, take up the full armor of God, so that you will be able to resist in the evil day, and having done everything, to stand firm."

[EPHESIANS 6:13]

As the days grew long and the weeks went by, I finally accepted the fact that I wasn't going home any time soon. This was not only a new year but also a new chapter in my life. God was showing me how to be tougher than tough, stronger than strong, and braver than brave. I had to be. I was in the Army now and had to accept what God allowed.

"Mack," my drill sergeant called out, holding up an envelope during mail call.

My mom wrote me every day. She kept my spirits high by encouraging me with scriptures and telling me to hang on to God's unchanging hand. She reminded me that everyone was praying for me. Occasionally, I would get a flood of letters from my church family. It made my fellow soldiers a bit envious. They didn't know that I needed those letters. While they were hanging out on the weekends, I would be on my bunk writing everyone back.

Things were yet intense and challenging, but I took the advice my sister gave me in one of her letters to "make the best of a bad situation." By this time, I had received my first paycheck. Entering as a private, my check was less than I received working part-time at Taco Bell and Hudson's. It was less than $200, but I used every bit of it to purchase writing materials, stamps, feminine products, and snacks at the Post Exchange, which we called "The PX." It was similar to a local Rite Aid or Walgreens. One thing that lifted my spirits was the fact that the PX had scented lotions. Since all of my perfume sets were confiscated, I looked forward to having a smell.

NO ORDINARY DRILL SERGEANT

Drill Sergeant Johnson worked with us a lot. She was as mean as a junkyard dog. The only bones she seemed to be hungry for were mine. I was relieved when I was assigned to Drill Sergeant Green. He had a gift for calling cadence. His voice made you forget how hot or tired you were. His uniforms were so crisp that you could hear the starch when he led us in a march. As you looked down at his boots, you could see your reflection in his spit shine.

"Which one of you privates are stinking up my formation?"

He sniffed every rank until he found the culprit. "Mack! Is that you wearing perfume in my formation?" I told him the truth that I wasn't wearing perfume, but he wasn't convinced.

"If I can smell you, the enemy can too! So, I suggest you wash whatever that is off at once."

I didn't see the big deal. I mean, we weren't in battle, and… it wasn't perfume.

NO ORDINARY COMPULSION: WEEKS 1 TO 3

Everything I learned during the following weeks taught me discipline and helped build teamwork. I knew there was a purpose behind every area of training. I just hoped there was a nicer way to do it. Nonetheless, I conformed.

The first thing I had to do was retake my PT test. I was happy to have met the requirements for the pushup event. I surpassed the expectations in the situp event again but failed the run by about 40 seconds. It might have sounded close, but in the Army, being close isn't good enough. All of the running, marches and fitness training helped me as time passed. As disappointing as it was to be in the remedial training group, I excelled in everything else. I memorized the Army's core values. I mastered disassembling, reassembling, and caring for my M16 rifle. I even kicked butt in the hand-to-hand combat exercises.

When it came to barracks inspections, everything had to be spaced, folded, and hung properly in my wall lockers. My bunk had to be made, tucked, and pulled tight enough for a quarter to bounce off of. If anything was off by a hair or something was missing, I'd be in for a treat. My drill sergeant was so impressed by the order of my locker that he used it as an example. I think that was the start of my Obsessive-Compulsive Disorder (OCD).

NO ORDINARY COMPULSION: WEEKS 4 THROUGH 5

During these weeks, we made special emphasis on weapons training. To some, the next phase was a dream. It was a bit more challenging for me, especially as a lefthander.

I began receiving fewer punishments and more compliments regarding my improvements. One exception was the time I kept moving in formation due to a bumblebee that continued to swarm around me.

"Private Mack, I don't care if that bee lands on your nose; you do not move in my formation. Now drop and give me 20!"

I made it past ten when Drill Sergeant Russell said, "Get up, Soldier!"

With his help, I qualified as a sharpshooter, which is one level below expert. I learned how to zero in on a target and fire dead on coming at various times and multiple ranges. By the time we finished the phase, I was an expert shooter.

One day, after practicing at the range, I finished early and turned in my ammunition. With all the map, compass, fitness, and night training, I must have been dead tired because I slept through chow and the last formation to return my weapon.

When my drill sergeant found me, he and the other drill sergeants let me have it. They yelled at me, embarrassed me in front of my entire platoon, and gave me extra duties, including fire guard and cleaning the barracks. It was the final straw. I'd had it! I did everything I was commanded, surrendered my will, and kept a positive attitude. I fought through tears and endured pain, even having to carry someone twice my weight that jumped on my back instead of letting me lift them to pull. I didn't care that I only had a few more weeks to go. I wanted out of the Army and NOW!

NO ORDINARY CONSUMPTION

I did my best to cry silently, but my battle buddy heard me in between sniffs. She tried consoling me, telling me things would get better. I didn't see how. Even after the nine weeks of basic training were up, I had orders to go to advanced training. There would be no immediate end. To make matters worse, I had only one more chance to pass the run on my physical fitness test.

My emotions probably aided in the return of my menstrual cycle. With it came an intense migraine. The pain was unbearable. It was as if someone were stabbing me in my temple with a dagger. I wanted the pain to stop, but it was nothing I could do this close to lights out. When my battle buddy asked if there was anything she could do, I asked her if she had any aspirin. Thankfully, she had some pain killers – her definition of some, at least.

The PX didn't sell anything other than Tylenol and nothing stronger than extra strength, so I assumed that was what she had given me. In fact, that's what the label on the bottle read. Sadly, for me, it wasn't extra strength... and it wasn't Tylenol.

My battle buddy's bottle was nearly full. She told me to take as much as I needed for my pain. I took two of them at first. I don't know what came over me to cause me to consume more, but I did. After an hour of not feeling better, I took another two and another two. Suddenly, I started to feel strange. When you factor in the fact that I didn't eat dinner and took whatever this was on an empty stomach, I was in deep trouble; so was my battle buddy.

When I woke up, I was in a military hospital. I was asked a series of questions – my name, social, rank, and how many pills I had taken in the bottle. I answered to the best of my knowledge before being instructed to drink a nasty, gritty, black substance called Charcoal to rid my body of the medicine.

I was ambulanced back to the barracks, where I was placed in a room and watched 24-7 by various shift guards. They were told to wake me every hour to ask me the same questions: "Do you want to harm yourself? Do you want to harm others?"

I replied "No" each time. Still, I remained under surveillance.

The next day, I had to return to the hospital, but on a different floor. It was for mental patients. I had to prove that I didn't want to harm myself or others. To me, it was more frustrating than convincing people how I didn't know I had signed up to join the Army.

I was monitored like clockwork. I had to take medication that I refused at first. When they told me the longer I refused, the longer I would stay there, I decided to give in. It was the first time I wished I were back at the post for training.

Listening to the issues of various soldiers (some older, some younger), I realized that my life at this point wasn't as bad as I thought. The saying, "There's always someone worse off than you," proved true.

After three days, I asked if I could return to post. Both the veteran psychologist and psychiatrist approved my request on the condition that I sign a waiver stating I volunteered to be discharged from therapy. Without hesitation, I did.

NO ORDINARY RETURN

When I returned to boot camp, it was as if everything had changed. I had a new battle buddy, the drill sergeants treated me differently, and I, too, felt a bit strange. Yet, I was determined to finish strong.

The next day, I took my PT test. I decided to take it easy on the situps to save my leg muscles for the run. Although I was alone, I wasn't by myself. I prayed for God to help me, and He did. It was as if He had sent angels to encamp all around me. When I felt like stopping, He whispered, *"You can't afford to stop. Slow down if you must, but stopping is not an option."*

As I approached the three-quarter mark, my drill sergeant stepped out of the sidelines and ran beside me. He let me know my time and how much of it I had left. "Private Mack? If you keep the same pace as me, the finish line would be yours for the taking."

The closer I got, I could hear other soldiers in my platoon shouting my name and cheering me on. I couldn't believe how much they cared to see me win. I knew I had to, not just for me, but for everyone. I took deeper breaths, put on my ugly face, and gave it all I had. I somehow managed to pass my drill sergeant.

"That's it, Mack! HOORAH!"

I did it! With God's help and the encouragement of those before me, I passed all three categories.

NO ORDINARY PHASE

The final phase, weeks six through nine, was called the Warrior Phase. All the exercises and training we did were designed to build our individual tactical training, increase our leadership skills and self-discipline, and improve our understanding of teamwork.

We continued with advanced rifle marksmanship training. We maneuvered and engaged targets as a team. During one of the exercises, another soldier's shell grazed my ear and burned me. At the end of the day, I was a celebrated boot camp hero.

By this time, the drill sergeants delegated or asked for volunteers to lead morning PT exercises, marches, and cadence calling. The next morning in formation, I was nominated to lead a couple of cadences in our first five-mile march. I sang like I was back home in the choir.

Mama Mama, can't you see what's this Army's done to me.
Mama Mama, don't you cry; your little girl ain't gonna die.
Oh oh oh oh, oh oh oh yeah, oh Lord, I wanna go.

It was time to put all my training together to pass the final test. And I did. Now, it was time to celebrate.

NO ORDINARY GRADUATION

Army basic training graduation was like nothing I had seen before. This final week was all about our families and us. After we finished the final training events (one week of field training and a ten-mile march back to post), we received a day with our families to catch up on our experiences.

The word "happy" is an understatement to describe the feeling I felt when I saw my mom. She came bearing gifts. She surprised me by bringing my sister (who was about eight months pregnant) and my little nephew. I couldn't believe it. I was able to go off post and enjoy time with them. I told them all about my successes, scary moments, and funny moments. Both my mom and sister were proud of me. Although my nephew was only one-year of age, I felt he was excited for me too.

The next day, I prepared for graduation. My mom had already sent me hair supplies, including a curling iron in a care package. I used it to give myself curls on the side with a French Twist in the back. I knew Drill Sergeant Johnson would be eyeballing me to ensure I followed the guidelines of my head gear fitting properly – something she made a point to do throughout my training. So, I did a trial run mirror check. I was good to go.

All the soldiers and I put on our dress uniforms with pumps. We had taken pictures in them to ensure a proper fit and took the time to ensure our rank, nameplates, and medals were properly polished and aligned.

When we marched in formation, our families clapped, cheered, and cried joyfully. We were not supposed to break rank by waving back or smiling, but I couldn't help it. I waited months to see my family. I was too full of emotion. When my eyes caught my mom's, I smiled and mouthed the words, *"Hi, Mom!"*

It was the last time I would see her before moving on to my next phase of training.

19 *Ninety-Five still*

AIT (Advanced Individual Training) was no ordinary development. It required more training, focus, time, and discipline. Here, I would learn the skills needed to perform my specific Army job as a combat medic. This was the time God showed me how to be on the front line of the battlefield, both physically and spiritually.

The Army's medical base was in Fort Sam Houston, Texas. I felt as if I had left crazy weather for extremely hot weather. It was the place I would spend the next 16 to 68 weeks. I learned a lot of the hands-on skills needed to succeed as a combat medic. As silly as it sounded, I didn't realize I would have to work with needles and see blood. I would never have agreed to work in such a field of study.

I learned basic first aid, CPR, trauma medicine, and wound care. I practiced on dummies for most practice exercises, such as applying tourniquets and treating shock victims. Then, on other soldiers regarding IVs and dressings for wounds.

Things were less stressful in AIT. We had larger barracks and larger platoons. We did more things together like talking at chow and were given more freedom, like drinking soda after our required two glasses of water at each meal. With that freedom came more responsibilities. There were more rank inspections where you are in formation and examined head to toe, ensuring your uniform is perfect with proper ranking, your headgear is on properly, and your boots are shined. Also, you would be asked questions at any given moment, such as who is your Command Sergeant Major or what are your Army core values? If you messed up, the consequences were still the same… "Drop and give me 20!" In other cases, you would have to fall to the rear of the chow formation. In Texas, with the size of our company after training along with the size of my appetite, I would say, "Houston, we have a problem!"

That was the drive that kept me on my toes. I stayed on top of my studies for combat medic school and basic Army values. As a result, I was chosen to be a squad leader. I oversaw ten soldiers, ensuring they stayed on top of things by offering my help and encouragement as needed. If I learned something to benefit me, I shared it with my squad. If one of us struggled, we all struggled and pulled together to push them to excellence.

One time, a soldier in my squad arrived late to formation. My drill sergeant, Drill Sergeant Wiggins, didn't make the guy drop and push it out. He made me drop and give him 20. When I looked around, my entire squad was knocking out the pushups with me. We were a team.

On the weekends, we could chill on base. We had a PX and a hang-out spot called La Hacienda. It was a lounge where we had the opportunity to unwind and have a structured level of fun. There, I learned how to shoot pool or play the game of Spades. Another area was a movie theater. Then, there were areas to order pizza and play arcade games.

NO ORDINARY UNIFORM

The Battle Dress Uniform (BDU) was no ordinary attire. We had summer and winter BDUs. Besides knowing they were designed to camouflage us in the field against the enemy, we had only learned how to roll our sleeves up or fill our pockets with necessary items. In AIT, we were also happy to have the opportunity to get them pressed and starched like the drill sergeants. But that's not all our BDUs could do. They were no ordinary uniform.

I never quite learned how to swim in high school, but I knew how to use a floaty. So, during one of our training exercises, we were told to wear our PT shorts underneath our uniforms. We were then instructed how to use our BDU pants as a floatation device and survival technique to prevent us from tiring out until help arrived.

NO ORDINARY NEWS

Calling home every week was my highlight. I would call my mom's, sister's, or maternal grandmother's house.

"Hello, Nuke," my grandmother would say with such a pleasant voice.

She was no ordinary grandmother. She was sweet as pie and as beautiful as the morning sky. She always smelled of flowers because she worked in her huge garden nearly every day. Afterward, she would bathe and dab on puffs of Shower to Shower body powder. I loved burying my nose in her neck just to smell her.

She had fair skin and super long, wavy hair that she would ask me to brush and style for her. I was her television show buddy. Before the news, we would watch Family Feud, Jeopardy, and Wheel of Fortune. In the summer, my mom let me spend the night for us to watch our yearly episodes of *Anne of Green Gables*.

Before I left for the Army, her eyesight began failing her. It was a side effect of the many things she endured as a diabetic. It made my heart happy to call her and hear her voice while I was in Texas. That's why I stopped everything I had to do to get back to Michigan when I heard the terrible news that she was on life support.

"Private Mack, you have an important message to call home."

I couldn't think of why I would have to call home. Surprisingly, sickness or death was the furthest thing from my mind because I was fortunate not to have dealt with either of these things in my family. When I found out my grandmother had an incident while on the dialysis machine, my mom asked if I could come back home before things worsened?

"I'll be there," I pledged.

I had no idea how I wasn't going to fulfill my promise. I just knew I had to get back home. I began by talking to my drill sergeant. He sent me to headquarters, where I had to wait a while to get approved, considering my grandmother was not immediate family. So, I prayed while I waited. When my time was up there, I received approval to travel off post to a connected travel company. The travel agency found me a flight that left within a couple of hours, but it cost me an arm and both my legs. The bad news was that I had to return in three days.

Leaving at this time was crucial. I was close to the end of my 16 weeks of training. Before graduating and being sent to my duty station, I had to spend time in the field, putting all my medical training into practice. If I didn't return in time, I would not be able to graduate with my class and would be considered a holdover, waiting for the next cycle of trainees to start over.

I chose to go home. I would only miss the first two days of field training if I returned in three days. I figured I could make it up.

NO ORDINARY EXIT

I had minutes before the taxicab driver arrived on base to take me to the airport. Other than the dress suit I arrived with at reception, I didn't have any civilian clothes I could travel in. Traveling in our BDUs was prohibited, so I put on the next best thing.

Traffic was crazy. I had less than 40 minutes to check in, go through an inspection, and find my gate.

The heavens were smiling down on me that day because I made it in the nick of time, sandals and all, with a huge Army green duffle sack on my back.

I was the last one boarding the plane heading to Detroit, Michigan. I didn't care about the eyes of aggravated passengers looking at me. My only concern was getting home to see my grandma.

NO ORDINARY LANDING

When my plane landed in Detroit, I felt a sense of hope come over me. It made me forget all about what I was wearing because I waited months to return home, though I wished it had been under different circumstances. Once my mom recognized me, she grabbed me close and squeezed me tight. It was the best welcoming present I could receive. She was happy to have me back home when she needed me most.

NO ORDINARY VISIT

I arrived late that day, so I wasn't able to see my grandmother that night. The next day, getting to her was the only thing on my mind. I didn't make this trip to catch up on all the things and people I left behind months prior. My mission was to see my grandmother, pray for her, and watch God turn her situation around. Sadly, she was in an intensive care unit which only allowed her one to two visitors at a time. Being that she had six children (including their spouses and children) in addition to a husband, sister, and sister-in-law all living in Flint, my chance of seeing her was slim to none. I yet attempted before visiting hours were over.

When I arrived at the hospital, I saw some of my aunts and uncles and a few of my cousins. The look on their faces told me that things were worse than I thought. My heart skipped a beat.

I was given a couple of minutes to enter her room before the nurse returned to do her rounds and handle her intensive care needs. I hoped to be with her alone, but time wouldn't allow it.

When I saw her, she was hooked to a breathing machine. She also had an IV attached to her. There were other bags attached to her and machines near her that were beeping in a rhythmic pattern. As if those things weren't scary enough, she didn't even look like the woman I knew. Her hair was curly – a way she never liked it. Her lips were dark. Her complexion was dark as well. She was swollen. She was lifeless.

I didn't want to cry to show that I had no hope or to add to the pain my mom and family were already going through. So, I stroked her hair. I kissed her forehead and said, "I love you, Gram. This is your favorite granddaughter, Nuke. I came all this way just to see you." After I spoke these words, my aunt told me it was time for me to go.

NO ORDINARY REQUEST

I changed clothes later that day and went to the best place I could go at the time – church. When I arrived at the start of the service, everyone was so excited to see me. I was there for the part I wanted to participate in the most: the prayer.

I didn't take up time to share everything I had gone through. I thanked God for traveling mercies and appreciated my mom, family, and everyone who sent me letters, cards, and care packages. Lastly, I requested prayer for my grandmother.

That night, I got down on my knees and prayed like I hadn't prayed before. I was happy to be able to do it freely in my own bedroom.

NO ORDINARY LOSS

I awakened the next morning feeling revived. It was as if God had given me confirmation that I would receive some news on this day. After eating breakfast, my sister let me know that she would come with me to the hospital.

When we got there, we were met by a couple of family members who directed us to enter a private waiting room within the hospital where more of our relatives were gathered. I hugged as many as I could. Most were smiling and happy to see others they hadn't seen in a while. Others were anticipating good news.

When the door to the waiting room opened, there was nothing but silence. The decision was made to pull the plug. My grandfather, aunts, and uncles all got up to leave the room and see my grandmother for the last time. I thought we would be allowed to do the same, but we weren't. All the cousins huddled, cried, and mourned for the glue that kept our family together for 62 years. This was no ordinary loss.

I knew the funeral would soon follow, but how could I return to serve in Uncle Sam's Army now? I didn't want to, and I made up in my mind that I would not be making a trip back to Texas. I didn't care about how far I had come or all I had endured up until this point.

My mom asked me when my flight was expected to leave the next morning. I said, "I don't know, and I don't care."

She said, "Jamillah, I need to know so I can take you to the airport." I didn't care about flight information or anything that didn't involve the current situation, so I said, "I'm not going back, Mom. I'm staying here with you."

NO ORDINARY LEAVE

My mother couldn't believe the words that had fallen from my lips.

"What do you mean you're not going back? You can't stay here. That's called going AWOL.! The military police can show up anytime, and you can be in an Army prison."

In my opinion, I was already in prison. But she was right. I had already been through enough. I didn't want to put myself through more turmoil, so I packed, found my flight information, and prepared to return to Texas.

On the plane, I found my seat and stared out the window. I was numb inside. I couldn't believe what had just happened. Before I knew it, I let out a wail. I wanted my grandma back. I wanted to hug and smell her one last time. No one heard me because I was in the rear of the plane.

Once I landed, I caught a cab back to base. When I arrived, the barracks were empty. I soon found out that I had not made it back in time. My unit had left for the field (the next step before graduating from AIT). I had come back for nothing. I would soon be a holdover, having to wait weeks until the next cycle of troops to restart another 16 weeks of advanced training.

That night, after hearing the shocking news following the death of my American idol, I lost control. While taking my shower, my tears blended in with the fall of the water. My cry mixed with the sound of the steam fan, and my knees buckled. Before I knew it, I was in a hurled position on the shower floor.

19 Ninety-Seven

A couple of years had gone by. I finished my training in Texas but found it difficult to deal with the consequences of being held back as a result of starting over. This was the year I had to make a conscious decision to keep living under the radar or serve my time. God helped me make the best decision to serve Him and honor my commitment to Uncle Sam.

So much time had transpired between restarting as a holdover that I stopped reporting for duty. I didn't talk to anyone. I felt ashamed to let my family know that I had basically gone AWOL. At one point, I couldn't go back to base without risking the punishment of being away. Therefore, I had no place to stay.

One of my drill sergeants saw me and asked me what was going on. After briefly sharing my dilemma, he had compassion and offered me a place to stay. He and his roommates lived off base. They would be away in the field for roughly 30 days at a time. That gave me a small window of cushion to crash at their place rent-free. What I didn't know was how filthy they lived. How could the same men who pounded us with discipline, cleanliness, and order live like slobs? It was a shocker! Nonetheless, I had no other option.

While they were away, I cleaned their entire quarters. I had it smelling like Mr. Clean and Mrs. Pine-Sol. Their once black-stained shower and tub were transformed back to their original beauty. The refrigerator and kitchen became a place someone would want to eat out of again. When they returned, they couldn't believe their eyes or noses.

Word spread about the great job I had done, and to make ends meet, I began cleaning living quarters for male soldiers who lived off base. It was a dirty job. As time passed, I knew I could no longer stay when the men returned from the field, and I couldn't continue cleaning homes for those soldiers who wanted to offer me more than a tip for my services.

NO ORDINARY DECISION

I had a decision to either face my punishment in the Army Reserve or go Active Army. Although the founder of my local church had one of his daughters write a letter of explanation for me to be released from the military, it was too late for a positive outcome due to the consequences of my previous actions. I accepted my fate and decided to finish the remainder of my time on active duty.

I didn't think I would ever get through it, but I remembered I had gone through worse. To make the decision easier, I was able to choose a new military job. My boyfriend (at the time) convinced me to be stationed near him. That's why I chose to be a transportation coordinator. It wasn't something I cared much for, but I was guaranteed a position in Georgia. Unfortunately, I had to first train in Fort Bragg, North Carolina, before making it to Georgia, followed by Fort Eustis, Virginia.

NO ORDINARY FORT

Fort Bragg was not a place I would *brag* about, but it was definitely better than Fort Leonard Wood, Missouri, and Fort Sam Houston, Texas. It was one of the largest military installations in the world. I was educated on everything I needed about being a Transportation Coordinator – a high-demand job.

From Fort Bragg, I furthered my training in a joint base with the Army and Airforce called Langley-Eustis in Hampton, Virginia. It was like an Army college life – more relaxed. When my training in Fort Eustis was complete, I was stationed in Georgia near Fort Stewart, called Hunter Army Airfield (HAAF). I was super excited to arrive because it was a big change for me. It was to be my permanent duty station. I looked forward to the sense of stability. It was an infantry battalion. To top it off, my location was considered a rapid deployment spot—meaning I would constantly be sent to areas where Uncle Sam needed me most. With my job being transportation, there was no escape.

Here, I learned how to change a tire, change oil, and drive a military-operated vehicle called a Humvee. These vehicles were built to serve one purpose, which wasn't for comfort. In addition, I worked on a flight line manifesting passengers and loading cargo on planes, boats, and automobiles. We stayed on alert for arriving flights.

NO ORDINARY LIVING QUARTERS

One of the things I enjoyed most was the responsibility and freedom I was given in a predominantly male field. Other than myself and my captain, there were only two other females. When one of the females became pregnant, it narrowed our unit down to three females. The female captain had separate sleeping quarters from us. So, it was no surprise that we had our own rooms. That alone boosted my morale, being some of the best news I had received in a long time. Unfortunately, though, we shared barracks with the male soldiers. It was bad enough having to get used to the locker room smell as we entered our barracks. We also had to share the laundry room. I didn't like anyone (especially guys) touching my clothes. Previously, if someone's things were finished washing and she hadn't returned, as a form of courteousness, another female would place them in the dryer for her. Not the guys! They would place our underwear or bras on their heads and parade around in them for all to see.

On the positive side, at least we didn't have to share shower rooms with them. Each room was divided by a bathroom. In a normal setting, that meant a maximum of four people to a bathroom. Given our unique circumstances, it was usually only two people in the sharing. I could deal with that. We had no ordinary arrangement: I kept the bathroom clean and smelling good; they kept us stocked on toiletries.

NO ORDINARY INSPECTION

Soldiers received the Battalion Commander's coin for the best room when a room was neat and clean. They expected nothing on the floor and things in their proper place. These were no ordinary inspections. They were either a surprise inspection or scheduled. Unlike in basic training, these were a little more relaxed. We didn't have to have our wall lockers and drawers dress-right-dress, but they had to smell and look decent with some form of organization. We no longer had to use the itchy Army green bedding.

I took the liberty to create a home away from home environment. I purchased a comforter set from the local Post Exchange (PX). I bought an extra set of sheets and some hooks to create a private canopy around my bed. That way, if I ever got a roommate, I would still have privacy. As an added touch, I painted my room. By the time the Command Sergeant Major (CSM) inspected my room, I had received his coin. Having the coin didn't come with any rewards or special privileges, but the thought of earning them gave me a sense of accomplishment. I seemed to receive one with every inspection. Not everyone was happy for me, but it didn't matter. I sucked at too many other things not to be given *these* moments to have *my* moments.

19 Ninety-Eight

NO ORDINARY SITUATION

*"But He was wounded for our transgressions,
He was bruised for our iniquities; the
chastisement for our peace was upon Him,
and by His stripes, we are healed."*

— [ISAIAH 53:5] —

I thought I had endured the worst of life. This was the year I learned how to keep loving God through all the hateful things I would soon face.

The Army was in a time of peace. After weekday work hours and even on the weekends, we could travel off post and enjoy time away from base. Just minutes from Savannah, it was such a quiet and beautiful place to be stationed.

I learned the ins and outs of duty station life and met new friends who would become family during my stay. I finally adjusted to the southern heat of Georgia and passed my PT tests. I was also promoted to Private First Class (PFC) and then Specialist in less time than most. My study skills and determination further earned me recognition as *Soldier of the Month* for three months in a row and *Soldier of the Quarter*. I was ready and focused on becoming *Soldier of the Year*. Overall, life seemed to be pretty good.

Being on my third or fourth rotation of roommates, I grew tired of giving out keys or having fresh ones made. They had a habit of losing their keys. It was the same with my newest roommate. When she decided to go out partying one evening, she asked if I could stay up and listen out for her. I had just come off of flight line duty and hadn't been to sleep in 24 hours. One of the guys suggested I leave the door unlocked for her, and I agreed. It sounded like the perfect idea.

Why didn't I just give her the key? In the worst-case scenario (if she had lost the key), we both would pay a $50 or $75 replacement fine. The guy's roommate who made the suggestion took it upon himself to sneak into my room. When I opened my eyes, I wished I were dreaming. I had a voice, but I couldn't speak. I had strength, but I couldn't fight. I was numb. He raped me!

The damages done to me that night were both internal and external. I wanted to die. I began questioning myself.

"Haven't you been through enough? When is this fight ever going to be over? Is God still with you?"

That same night, I found a knife in the sink. A voice in my head encouraged me to end it all. The more I tried to ignore it, the louder it became. So, I took in a deep breath and counted to three.

"One… (tears filled my eyes). Two… (tears rolled down my face). THREE!"

The knife didn't go in. It was as if God had sent an angel down to stop me. Feeling ashamed and grateful at the same time, I repented. I picked up the phone and called my spiritual father. I didn't have to tell him who I was. He already knew. I didn't explain what happened to me. God had already intervened. I only asked him five simple words, "Will you pray for me?" He prayed like never before. After crying myself to sleep that night, I was ready to expose my abuser.

When I reported the assault to my captain, I trusted that she would be discreet in handling the situation. I was wrong. Nothing was being done as far as I knew. I had to work with him, endure his winks, degrading comments, and smirks. No one believed he could do such a thing. He was well-liked in our unit. They figured, *"Why would he?"*

Days later, after experiencing some unordinary symptoms, I decided to go to sick call – a place similar to a local urgent care clinic. After taking samples, I was found to have an STD. I was given medication and a special shampoo. I was also encouraged to "share with [my] partner the information for him to get treated as well." The audacity. I was enraged. I wanted him to know what he had done to me.

Later that day, I told him I had reported him and what he had given me. When I went to my car, I found my tires slashed. Days later, I received orders to be deployed.

This was most definitely no ordinary situation. Why did I have to leave? I was months away from competing for *Soldier of the Year* – an achievement that would have awarded me free dry cleaning for a year, a brand-new car for a year, and the title itself.

I had 30 days to prepare and go through clearance – making sure all my affairs were in order, finding storage for my personal items (including car), and getting all the necessary vaccinations before departing. Within that time, I shared with my mom and sister the horrific news of the assault and the orders. I felt my mom's hurt, anger, and frustration through the phone. To help me during this trauma, I arranged for my sister to visit me. When she did, it gave me the shot in the arm I so desperately needed

19 *Ninety-Nine*

NO ORDINARY ORDERS

"A time to love, and a time to hate; a time of war, and a time of peace."

[ECCLESIASTES 3:8]

I wasn't just in a different state. I was in a different country. This was the year God literally took me out of my comfort/time zone. He showed me that no matter my location, He was omnipresent. I learned what it was like to take the Lord with me everywhere I went.

My deployment papers to Saudi Arabia were no ordinary orders. I had to learn their ways and customs – what not to wear, say, or do. I was there to maintain protection and trade relations.

The uniforms I had to wear in the desert were completely different from the ones worn stateside. They were tan. Instead of leather and black boots, I had suede and tan ones.

I first lived in a type of frat house for soldiers on base before moving to a tent in a remote, rugged desert camp. It was scary, to say the least. There were lizards, snakes, scorpions, and more. The water was harsh and undrinkable. I remember being asked if I had dyed my hair orange. The chemicals of my perm, along with the contents of the water, discolored my hair and made it brittle. The water even made my skin feel rough. To top it off, it was extremely hot!

Having the U.S. military personnel prepare most of our food was the upside. The downside was being unable to drink or brush our teeth in the running water. So, we used both locally produced bottled water and purified water.

To free our minds of the day-to-day stressors, we visited places on the camps. All the tents had themes. My tent was painted with the old cartoon actress Betty Boop wearing camouflage. There was a tent to have fun and watch television. One of my favorite tents was *31 Baskin Robins*. My other favorite was the Chapel. It didn't compare to my church back home, but having a place set aside to worship God kept me going. One day, I even volunteered to sing a song – *I Won't Complain*. As many times as I had heard it before stateside, the words touched my heart in ways I hadn't felt before.

NO ORDINARY WHEELS

I was given my own vehicle as a transportation specialist. It was a brand-new white Jeep. The cool part wasn't just the AC, but the steering wheel was on the right side of the car. In addition, I had to learn how to drive a stick shift. It was so unordinary. I was thankful I didn't have to drive on the opposite side of the road.

I also learned how to operate a forklift. I felt empowered riding it around in the scorching heat of the day. It didn't have AC, but the breeze (though hot) created moments of peace for me. We were losing soldiers left and right, hearing about tragic news all around. So, I found hope in the smallest of things. One of them was being able to email my mom daily and receive her emails more frequently than I would a letter.

NO ORDINARY LETTER

The availability of the phone booths was slim to none. If I did happen to secure one, the hopes of me reaching someone back home within the seven-hour time zone difference was nearly impossible. My best bet was writing. However, the turnaround time for our camp's postal service was about a five to six-day delay. That's why I wrote letters via email.

I got to a point where I didn't want to update my mom or anyone back home with any more bad news. I typed her an email that promised her that. And from that moment on, I remained positive no matter what I faced. Many times, we were in tough situations, having to carry our weapons with us even to the latrines (the military version of a porter potty). It didn't matter. I held on to the fact that somebody was praying for me and had me on their mind.

NO ORDINARY WAR

After serving six months in Saudi Arabia, I was able to go home for the Christmas holiday for a week. I was not prepared for what happened after we retrieved my luggage from the baggage claim. The coldness of winter struck me like an enemy on the battlefield. I immediately went into shock. I guess the drastic change of leaving 123-degree temperatures for months straight and coming to 40-degree temperatures would send anyone into distress. Even after my mom gave me her coat and a blanket and cranking up the heat to knock off the chill, I still quivered. We were 45 minutes into our drive home when I finally felt my body acclimate. I didn't survive the dangers of fighting in the Army just to travel all the way home and freeze to death.

I enjoyed my time home before being stationed in Kuwait. My dedication and determination helped get me promoted to staff sergeant. By now, I had earned my stripes. It was an honor that said I served at least three continuous years of service. It motivated me to do what God had authorized me to do. I no longer complained about why I was there, what happened to me, or how I was tricked into joining. It was all a part of His plan. I thanked the Lord for my past, embraced my present, and looked forward to my future. I was already fighting an unordinary war.

SGT. JAMILLAH LYNN
- WIFE & MOTHER
- TEACHER
- VETERAN
- FIRST LADY
- SURVIVOR

2 Thousand

"When I was a child, I spake as a child, I understood as a child, I thought as a child: but when I became a [woman], I put away childish things."

— [1 CORINTHIANS 13:11] —

This was the year God grew me. At twenty-five, I may have been another year older and a couple of inches taller, but I had also matured in my faith and finally found my purpose.

After returning stateside to Georgia for a couple of months, I received deployment orders to Egypt. I was mentally ready this time. I didn't complain or look for excuses as to why my previous issues and complaints were never addressed and brushed under the rug. Instead, I understood my assignment and accepted the call with honor.

My mindset was different. My outlook on life had changed. I felt the inward growth that life's experiences taught me. Now, I was ready for my 15-hour flight to Egypt.

This was probably the shortest of the international flights, but there were several stops and leg breaks. Each time, I made sure to purchase souvenirs for family and friends back home. I bought things like pens, refrigerator magnets, and t-shirts from Chicago, New York, Ireland, and anywhere there was a layover.

When I touched down in Egypt, it had to be around 0700 hours. I thought that being stationed in Saudi Arabia and Kuwait would prepare me for the sweltering heat of Egypt. Not so. It was unbearable even in the morning. It was like sticking my head in the oven at 225 degrees. I felt the heat walking through the tunnel to the airport, and I couldn't wait to sit under the air conditioning in my barracks.

NO ORDINARY BARRACKS

As I arrived on base, I saw soldiers from all over the world. The plethora of uniforms was exciting. People were walking; others were riding bikes. To my surprise, no one was driving vehicles. Having a bicycle was the way to get around. I purchased a bike from one of the soldiers who was getting ready to return stateside. It was one less thing they had to ship home, and it was one more thing I could use to help me get around camp.

Like before, the water was only safe enough to bathe in. The good news was that I didn't have to leave my barracks to shower or brush my teeth. These were no ordinary barracks. They were similar to an oversized trailer home. Inside, the females had their own barracks and own room. I liked it already. The only thing we had to share was the latrine (bathroom). I was happy with that, too, because we finally had doors. In Saudi and Kuwait, we had to walk outside to use an open shower room.

I jazzed up my room with some wall art and pictures I purchased at the PX to give it a homey feel. I had pyramid and Egyptian figurines with sheets hanging to separate my bed from my business side. On the business side, I had a small T.V. and a couple of chairs for a sitting area. It's where I would style or braid hair on the weekends for the other female soldiers on camp. Once word got out that I styled and braided my own hair, I stayed occupied on the weekends.

NO ORDINARY CREW

Here, I didn't work on the flight line. Instead, I was more of a liaison for all the military personnel on the campsite. I helped with travel, shipment of personal property, and documentation of soldier entitlements. I worked with 11 different contingents (Hungarians, Colombians, Fijians, Norwegians, Britains, etc.). For communication purposes, I had to learn the basics of their language. Overall, I enjoyed my job and the team I worked with. I was the youngest of two females and was treated like a little sister.

In our office or trailer were officers, sergeants, and specialists from around the world. We worked together to help all members of our workforce. At the end of the day, we respected one another's personal space, unique cultural backgrounds, and preferences. We learned new things about each other, like what kinds of foods we ate, popular songs, dances, and styles, along with traditions. It was important to know exactly who we were fighting together with. So, we took turns visiting someone's special event or traditional ceremony each week. These things helped boost our morale and kept us encouraged during difficult times.

NO ORDINARY GIFTS

Other things we did to appreciate each other was exchange gifts from our respected countries. Everyone liked our American shoes and clothes. Others would offer jewelry, paper, or music. When I traveled off base, I would purchase blankets, glass or metal pyramids, and other gifts to send home to family and friends.

One day, I observed a man painting a self-portrait. He did a phenomenal job. So, I asked him if he could paint a black and white portrait for me of my mother. He accepted and told me to come back in a few days. When I did, tears filled my eyes. It was one of the most beautiful things I had ever seen.

For myself, I ordered a silver necklace with a charm that had my name in English on one side. The opposite side was in Arabic. It was no ordinary gift. When the owner discovered my name, he asked, "Do you know what your name means?" Though I told him "Yes," he felt the need to explain. When I returned to pick up the necklace, the designer offered me his hand in marriage, saying I would be one of his wives and promising me a lifetime of gifts. I humbly declined.

NO ORDINARY TRAVEL ROUTE

On most weekends, I got to travel to Tel Aviv or Cairo. It was always scary. The roads alone were dangerous. There were no guard rails around hills and slopes. Also, if you did not reach your destination by a specific time of the day, the nights were pitch black. There were no lighted pathways or streetlights. We relied on our vehicle's headlights and flashlights. It was bad enough having to watch out for mines, but we also had to beware of innocent-looking children begging for food and water who were placed as decoys. We learned the hard way not to fall for it.

NO ORDINARY OBSTACLE COURSE

The wee hours of the day were still set aside for PT. Our training consisted of push-ups, flutter kicks, sit-ups, partner-assisted exercises, and company runs. The only difference was the turf and the temperature. By 0600 hours, it was already 100 degrees of dry heat. I always felt like I would pass out, but I pushed through it. On days when I had migraines, God always allowed them to come on after training where I could put an ice-cold compression on my forehead and rest. We stayed abreast of our rifle training and battle combative skills in the afternoons.

I was pretty good on the range. I could hit a target dead center, three shots in a row no matter the distance. I was also quick on the obstacle course, knowing how to get over a high wall without assistance and pull myself up using a rope. Those were probably two of the reasons I was nominated to represent the U.S. in a competitive obstacle course. It was similar to the Olympics for the military. It was an honor I gladly accepted.

Each team of five soldiers had a month of training in addition to their normal daily routines. My team chose to train at night when the temperature dropped to about 85 degrees. I liked it because we didn't have the heat of the sun beaming on us, but it didn't prepare us for the actual event.

On the day of the competition, our company commander gifted us with navy blue t-shirts with red lettering to represent our unit. The shirts read: "Without us, nothing moves!" They had the phrase above a truck on the front with our names inside stick faces on the back. To help keep me motivated, my sergeant made a fishing pole out of a broomstick with a string tied to it. At the end of the string (to represent the bait) was my all-time favorite – a Snickers bar.

Everyone on the campsite was there. I can't begin to describe the anxiousness and nervousness I felt. This was not to include the pressure from the temperature, which seemed to be the hottest so far.

The obstacle course began with a low wall (about five feet high) that we had to jump over using a sandbag. Second was a low crawl under some barbwire. Third were large rubber tires we had to muster our way through as quickly as possible before running and grabbing a rope to swing over a huge hole. I managed to grab hold of the rope and swing, but my hands were so wet from sweat that I slipped and hit my shin right on the corner of the hole before jumping off. It was painful. Still, I limped my way to the next obstacle, an inclined catwalk. After that, I had to swing over and crawl under a series of metal bars. I don't quite remember the other in-between obstacles, but I do remember the nine- or ten-foot-high wall.

My teammates were waiting for me because I was the anchor. They climbed on my back as I got down on all fours. Then, they placed their knees on my shoulders as I stood to help them over the wall, where the first person over pulled them up to jump down to the other side. After everyone made it over, I had to run, jump as high as I could and grab a rope left by the last person to climb over to the other side. Lastly, I ran to the final obstacle in the first part of the competition. It was a high rope. I climbed up a 15- or 20-feet long ladder with a rope in between connected to another log beam. The hard part was pulling myself across in full gear without turning belly up. It required strength and balance. To help, I was encouraged to hang one leg down and pull myself safely to the other side. I made it!

My team captain gave me a sip of water to cool me off for the second part – the one-mile run. So far, we were good on our time. I didn't want to let them know that I wanted to salute and call it quits at this point. It was hot. I was injured and hot. I was tired, injured, and HOT! I figured if I kept going, they would appreciate my attempt.

I started the run at a slow pace. About a quarter of a mile, I slowed down even more. Before I knew it, one of my teammates had loosened the straps to my Kevlar helmet and carried it for me to lighten my load. It only weighed about three pounds, but it was enough to give me a boost. I gave a nod of thanks and picked up the pace. Around the halfway mark, I began to slow down again. This time, another teammate said, "Mack! Give me your LCE!" An LCE (loading carrying equipment) was a belt that carried our canteens, ammunition, and other necessary items. I wanted to cry in appreciation, but I knew crying would make me hyperventilate and slow down more. Instead, I gave a thumbs up of thanks. They figured that we couldn't win the race without all the participants. They reminded me of my valuable role and that we were going to finish together. By the third quarter mark, I had picked up the pace more and felt my second wind. Before we finished the run, they handed my gear back to me so I wouldn't be disqualified, and we crossed the finish line.

We took a short water break and headed to the last and final event – the firing range. With dust in my eyes and dried sweat on my face, I gave it my best shot! I had to. This was my way of returning the favor for all my team had done for me during the run. God blessed me with a perfect score on the range, giving our team the maximum points. Then, after all the competing teams' points were calculated, we came in second place, representing well for the U.S. It was truly no ordinary victory.

2 Thousand still

NO ORDINARY SURPRISE

"Ask, and it shall be given you; seek, and ye shall find; knock, and it shall be opened unto you: For every one that asketh receiveth; and he that seeketh findeth; and to him that knocketh it shall be opened."

— [MATTHEW 7:7-8] —

The six months of being stationed in Egypt seemed like such a long time. I still had another six months to go. I was more than anxious, knowing that my time of military service would soon be over. This was the year God stunned me with some amazing news. He gave me what I needed instead of what I thought I wanted.

I saved up more than enough to be comfortable whenever I was discharged from the Army. I didn't plan on dipping into these funds early. But, when the question was asked if I would like to take a 30-day leave of absence, I didn't think twice. It was perfect timing because my close friend of nearly ten years was getting married. So, I put in the request, got approved, and began my search for the earliest and most cost-efficient flight home.

It was more challenging than I thought. After a long ride to the international airport, I had to go through clearance and customs. For security purposes, I understood the great lengths personnel had to go through to ensure the safety of our country, but I felt violated. This was in addition to the $2,000 round trip airline ticket I had to pay.

NO ORDINARY GENTLEMAN

Before I returned on this break, Edriece had gotten my mailing address overseas and written me a few letters and poems. I wrote him back. Still, I didn't think anything serious was brewing other than a friendship. Surprisingly, he asked me out to eat after church. We went to a restaurant called Kountry Kettle. They were about to close, so we just ordered dessert. He was cordial yet introverted. I thought, *"Why bother?"* I guess I enjoyed his company and how nice he was. I also liked the way he smelled and dressed too.

On his way to drop me off at home, he asked me to sing him a song. I sang a couple of verses from Take 6's *Join the Band* album called "It's Gonna Rain." He smiled and said he liked my voice. It gave me butterflies. We arrived at my home, and he parked his car on the street. We talked some more before he grabbed my hand and placed mine on top of his. As he gazed into my eyes, I just knew his next words would be as sweet and romantic as his poems. Instead, he said, "Do you know that you have big hands for a girl?" The butterflies left. I yanked my hand back and yelled, "GOOD NIGHT!" I couldn't believe him. That was no way to woo me. I didn't want to spend another minute with him. I didn't point out that his having a gold front tooth did not fit his personality. He had some nerve.

Three weeks had already gone by when he asked me out again. It was the night of my friend's wedding. After dropping me off and before walking me to the door, he asked to see my hand again. This time, he was trembling as he sang "Love Isn't Love" by Commissioned. The butterflies returned as he sang the words.

He got down on bended knee and asked me the magic words, "Will you marry me?" I wanted to say "Yes" instantly, but the words didn't come out. I extended my ring finger as he placed a beautiful Marquise cut diamond ring on it. I ran inside to tell my mother, who apparently already knew. She was happy for me. I was happy for me. It was no ordinary surprise. I spent as much time with him as I could during my last week home. Before I left, I tried giving him a passionate kiss. I figured it would be okay, given the circumstances. He pecked me and pulled away. I thought, *"This is no ordinary gentleman."*

2 Thousand One

Tina Turner sang it best – *What's love got to do with it?* It has a lot to do with it. The key was to stop searching for *it* and allow *it* to find me. When I did, God gave me the desires of my heart. This was the year He allowed me to be someone's good thing.

NO ORDINARY ENGAGEMENT PERIOD

The saying is true: "God will bless you with your hero after you let go of your zero." My hero asked me to marry him, and I was more than ready. By now, I had less than three months before being honorably discharged from active Army to return home to finish my time in the Army

114

reserves. I made sure to purchase as many callings cards as possible because someone new had been added to my list – my fiancé, Edriece.

We had no ordinary engagement period. Most people learn one another by dating and spending one-on-one time with each other. Edriece and I got to know each other through phone calls and letters. I enjoyed receiving and reading his letters and poems, which were more romantic than his friendlier ones. He had such nice handwriting. He would tell me about his ambitions and dreams as I shared with him my desire to return to school and receive my degree.

Back home, my sister helped organize my wedding party and design my wedding dress while my mom worked on making it. Edriece put in extra hours to pay for our honeymoon. He also got to know my mom and sister better by making them his signature pies. He was "The Man." I loved every bit of it. By the time I arrived home from Egypt, the only things we had left to do were talk to his pastor for marriage counseling, find a home, and get our blood work done.

NO ORDINARY HOME

Edriece had his share of apartment life, so he had no intentions of us moving into one as husband and wife. Therefore, we searched diligently for rental homes. It was no ordinary search because he wanted to stay on the south side of Flint, whereas I liked the north side. I had no issue compromising.

We searched every day. Most of the homes within our budget were not to our satisfaction. The ones that were pleasing to our taste were not on the south side. Finally, we found the perfect house and location. It was a small, yellow one-bedroom house with an open porch. It had a nice-sized backyard that made up for the house's small square footage. Edriece called it a "shotgun house" – you could see the back door from the front door.

He wanted more for me. He thought I was settling. I assured him that I was happy and could make the house a home with a little TLC. We cleaned the house from top to bottom, putting wallpaper and a ceiling fan in our bedroom. The wallpaper actually made our bedroom appear even smaller, and the ceiling fan was just inches above the mattress. It was just right for the two of us.

The living room had a large furnace in the corner, which made sounds at night. The bathroom was probably the largest room in the entire house, but the tub and shower were scary. Edriece and his cousin retiled it to make it look less frightening. Edriece cut the grass while I trimmed and edged the many bushes surrounding the house. As a finishing touch, I loaded his car with a ton of rocks I purchased from a cement company to make a rock garden. We would have a special place to live after the wedding.

NO ORDINARY TRAIT

His pastor talked to us about communication, keeping God first, and yielding to one another. It was all necessary.

Before setting up the appointment to get our blood work and medical exams, I shared with Edriece what physically happened to me in the Army. I didn't want any surprises or a marriage with secrets. So, I told him I would understand if he didn't want to go forward with the marriage. It didn't change how he felt about me. It was as if he grew a deeper love for me.

The biggest challenge came when we found out each of us had sickle cell trait – a condition in which a child receives the sickle cell gene from one parent. Although we didn't have the disease, together, we had a 25% chance of passing it on to our children. Knowing the pain associated with the disease, we had a lot to consider. After fasting and praying, we asked and trusted God that none of our children would have the disease. We then moved forward with the marriage.

NO ORDINARY FEET

Two months before the wedding, I somehow managed to get cold feet. I began thinking about how long I was away from home. How would I know if I could be a good wife and finish school at the same time? Would I be a good cook? At the time, the only things I knew how to cook were breakfast and Ramen noodles. Would I be a good mother to our children? I listened to the questions people kept asking me over and over: "Are you sure you're ready for marriage? Don't you want some time to find yourself first?" Maybe I did. The questions made me second guess myself. Not wanting to play with his emotions, I gave him his ring back.

NO ORDINARY DREAM

When word got out that the wedding was off, old flames and ex-boyfriends came out of the woodworks to express their so-called undying love for me. It wasn't that I was available; I wanted to be sure. I even asked my mom what she thought. Then, I remembered a conversation we had a year or so ago regarding a dream she had about me getting married. A year later, Edriece had proposed to me.

"Mom, remember the dream you had a while ago about me getting married? You talked about how beautiful the venue was, how packed it was, how happy I was, and how lovely the dress was. Was the man I married in your dream Edriece?"

I wished I had asked her sooner. Anyone who knows my mom understands she is a dreamer. Whenever she dreams about something or someone, you best believe it will come to pass.

"I can't answer that for you," she said. "But, if you rephrase the question, I will attempt to answer it."

Edriece had a gold front tooth when I first met him. He had an old football injury in high school where he cracked his front tooth. He told me that he couldn't afford to get a porcelain tooth at the time, so getting a root canal with a gold tooth was the least expensive route. He yet had this gold tooth when he proposed to me. So, I rephrased the question.

"Mom, did the man in your dream have a gold front tooth?"

She calmly replied, "No."

No? How could this be? If the man in the dream didn't have a gold tooth, it couldn't be Edriece. I was devasted. Without sharing this with him, I went into straight prayer mode before giving him an answer to whether or not we would give love another shot.

NO ORDINARY LOVE

There's nothing ordinary about love. There's puppy love, selfless love, the love of family and friends, the love between God and man, and the love between man and woman. I strongly believe that being wanted by many men will never compare to being valued by just one.

I've heard the saying: "If you love something, let it go. If it comes back, it's yours forever. If it doesn't come back, it wasn't meant to be." Maybe I wasn't *in* love with Edriece yet, but I truly loved him, and he loved me. He fought for me. He pursued me, even after I let him go. It wasn't long before he came back. It was certainly meant to be.

I had to go with my gut feeling on this one. I couldn't focus on my mom's dream. Edriece was the man for me. When he came over and proposed again, I said, "Yes!" The wedding was back on, and we had a short time to reorganize and get the ball rolling. We set a date for August 18th in honor of the founder's wife of my church.

NO ORDINARY DRESS

The day before my wedding, my mom and I purchased an arch for the designer to decorate. Afterward, I went to a nail salon to get my nails done. It was the first time I had done something like that. It made me feel special.

That night, my mom had a final fitting with all the ladies in my wedding party. She made their dresses as well as mine. When I tried mine on, it was a perfect fit, and I loved it. It was no ordinary dress. It had two layers. The bottom layer was a silky white dress with short sleeves. I wore a puffy loop and petticoat underneath to make it flair out. The top layer was a heavier material. The beautiful white swirls gave it a look of elegance. It had a super long train. It was a v-neck with a string of pearls outlining the collar. The sleeves were my favorite part. It was my sister's idea to have a four-inch slit at the bottom of the sleeve with strings of beads draping down my hand.

On the morning of my wedding, my sister washed and styled my hair in curls. We ate a delicious brunch and headed to the church early. I heard of weddings starting late, and I emphasized how I wanted mine to be one of the first to start on time.

The coordinator arrived late. It caused my mom to be pulled from doing what mothers and daughters do. She organized the food for the reception, the wedding party and made and set up the cake. Minutes before three o'clock, the coordinator arrived, and the wedding started on time.

I had a long wedding party which included junior bridesmaids and junior groomsmen. It seemed like an eternity before my sister whispered the words, "Are you ready? It's time."

As I walked down the aisle, my heart beat like thunder. I felt my emotions bubbling. I told myself, *"Don't cry. It's a happy occasion."* I made it halfway down the aisle when I could no longer fight back the tears. People were admiring my dress. "You look so beautiful, Jamillah."

When I reached the front of the altar, my handsome husband-to-be waited in an all-white suit. I could tell he was nervous the way he gave a half smirk. Just like my mom said in her dream, it was a beautiful venue, standing room only, and Edriece didn't have a gold tooth. He surprised me by replacing it with a nice porcelain one. I couldn't believe it!

I couldn't believe someone chose me and thought I was worth spending the rest of his life with. It was no ordinary union, a match made in heaven.

2 Thousand Two

While Edriece worked a nine to five, I continued to pursue my degree. I missed him the moment he left the house and couldn't wait to see him for lunch or anytime we had a break together. It was new to us, trying to build a life together. He was humble and reserved; I was stubborn and outspoken. He was an introvert; I was an EXTRA extrovert. It took time for me to adjust and yield to him as the head of the household. There were times I stormed out of the house. Sometimes, I even used the "D word" (divorce) if I couldn't get my way. Yet, at the end of the day, we found ourselves praying together, forgiving one another, and trying to understand each other.

We found happiness in the smallest of things. We ate dinner together every night. He didn't complain about my limited cooking skills. We laughed together, watching the same VCR movies over and over on his small television set. We didn't have much – no cable, no basement, or furniture. What we had was each other.

A month after we married, the nation heard the devastating news surrounding the 9-11 events. We soon found out some news of our own. God was adding to our union. He blessed me to carry our first child – a beautiful daughter.

NO ORDINARY POSITION

We moved into a larger two-bedroom home. By now, I was 40 weeks and two days. Since I didn't dilate past two centimeters, I was sent home. To help ease my comfort, I asked Edriece to drop me off at my mom's house. When I arrived, I fell to my knees and buried my head in her lap.

"Breathe in, breathe out," my mom whispered to me as she rubbed my back. I practiced the Lamaze breathing while keeping a soft song in my head to help deal with each contraction.

"Mama, something ain't right!" My mom toiled with me until it was time for her to go to work. She and my husband worked minutes from one another, so often they would carpool. This day, I asked her to drop me off at the hospital on her way to work. When I arrived at the hospital, they checked my cervix and said I was six centimeters dilated. The ultrasound showed that my daughter was breech.

NO ORDINARY BIRTH

"Jamillah, we have to give you an emergency c-section."

I was eight centimeters when the nurses came to wheel me down for surgery. On my way into the cold room full of surgeons, nurses, and interns, along with an anesthesiologist, I saw my mom, who helped ease my worries. She said, "Your hubby is here too. They're getting him ready."

The moment I couldn't feel anything from my belly button down, they brought my husband into the room. Seeing him was comforting. He kissed my forehead, wiped my tears, and said, "I know, Baby. It's going to be alright." After minutes of pulling, tugging, whispering, and yanking, out came my precious baby. They lifted her to show my husband before taking her to get cleaned up, checked over, and weighed. I asked him one question: "Does she have any hair?" She was the most precious thing I ever laid my eyes on.

NO ORDINARY SQUEAL

My husband and I were extremely concerned with how fast our daughter breathed. We were assured that it was normal, especially with babies delivered by c-section. It continued even after we were discharged home.

That night at around 3:00 a.m., she let out a squeal and began breathing slowly while I nursed her. I immediately called my mom. She asked me a series of questions and helped calm me down. When my daughter seemed to be comfortable, I went back to sleep.

The next morning, my husband told me he was going to church. He explained how his mother would be on her way to help care for the baby and me. I said, "I don't know her. Please don't leave me." He kissed me and assured me that he wouldn't be gone long.

The moment his mother came through the door, she frowned and stated, "Driece, that baby don't look right!" She grabbed her out of my arms and took her to the baby changing table for me to get some clothes on her. I tried lifting my daughter's leg. It fell limp. I tried lifting her arm. It fell limp. My daughter laid there lifeless. She had turned blue and stopped breathing.

My mother-in-law grabbed my daughter, placed her in the car seat, put her in her truck, and said, "Meet me at Hurley!"

I did my best to process everything. Could the very child I waited nine months to see enter this world only to leave days later? I had to soldier up and trust God. I ignored the pain I was feeling from my surgery and threw on some clothes as my husband helped walk me to the car.

He was calm. He didn't speak a word. I wondered, *"Why in the world is he this reserved?"* Then, it dawned on me. He was praying. He showed unordinary strength. It was internal. He was strong, brave, and courageous.

Before arriving at the hospital, he called our pastor and shared the news. The pastor said a word of prayer and later joined us. We met my mother-in-law in the ER.

NO ORDINARY SIGHT AND FLIGHT

My mother-in-law had retired from Hurley Hospital, so she knew what to do and say to get my daughter the fastest and best care possible. She burst through double doors and surpassed triage protocols to get her seen. Within minutes, my daughter was taken back and placed in a room. We couldn't accompany her. We had to trust that God placed her in good hands.

Our precious angel had IVs, needles, and tubes everywhere as she was hooked to a breathing machine. They explained that she had two holes in her heart (an atrial septal defect and a ventricular septal defect) along with coarctation of the aorta that prevented blood from flowing properly. She needed surgery, and she needed it fast. She was medevacked to Detroit Children's Hospital by an emergency team. We wasted no time packing our things before joining them.

NO ORDINARY SURGEON

So many people were calling, praying, and sending their love for us during this difficult time. Along with their love were monetary donations to help offset financial burdens. We were fortunate to stay in the Ronald McDonald housing.

A person that stood out was the surgeon. He came in to explain the procedure and the risks involved. After handing him the signed consent forms, the most unusual thing happened. He asked, "Can I pray with you all?" Our precious gift, Imari, was put in the hands of someone who put their hands in God's.

The surgery was a success! The team continued feeding Imari intravenously with milk I had pumped and stored until I could nurse her again. Within three months, we were able to take her home. It was no walk in the park. She required 24-hour care and constant monitoring. God helped us through it all.

2 Thousand Five

> ### NO ORDINARY UNDERSTANDING
>
> *"Trust in the Lord with all thine heart, and lean not unto thine own understanding. In all thy ways acknowledge him, and he shall direct thy paths."*
>
> — [PROVERBS 3:5-6] —

A year after Imari was born, my Army reserve unit was alerted. The Lord knew I didn't want to leave my husband and baby behind, but I had to fulfill my commitment. I would have to notify my university of a leave of absence and follow through with my orders. All female soldiers had to take a pregnancy test before deployment. My positive test excused me from being sent to Afghanistan. Four months later, I miscarried. It was devastating, especially after announcing the news to family, friends, and coworkers. Before long, we were blessed with our son, Junior, in 2004.

A year later, my reserve unit was called to serve again. My pregnancy test results were positive. Four months later, on the day we were to find out the gender, we learned I had another miscarriage. I tried wrapping my head around things. I knew God wouldn't put more on me than I could bear. Maybe the two miscarriages had sickle cell disease, or perhaps if I weren't pregnant, I would have been killed in the war. I realized it was all a part of God's plan. Like Déjà vu, I knew God specialized in doing it again. This is the year I leveled up naturally and spiritually by trusting God's timing. I had to set aside my own understanding and lean towards His.

NO ORDINARY DEGREE

Most people who love math go into the field of science. I had a love for math and fine arts. To combine this unordinary field of study, I pursued an arts and science degree. It wasn't easy. I fought hard to obtain a 3.500-grade point average (GPA) and even harder to maintain it. My sudden departure to join the Army left me with unsatisfactory grades. I dropped down to a 3.0 and left with a 2.5. I had to petition to turn those grades into incompletes and to have other courses dropped off my record. Doing so left me with a 1.500. Once approved, I worked diligently to receive high enough markings to improve my grade point average. Every marking period, God blessed me to receive a 4.000. When I graduated, I earned high honors and my initial GPA of 3.500. It was no ordinary celebration.

NO ORDINARY ROUTINE

As with my births, I had to push through the pain of working, going to school, and being a full-time mom and wife. I couldn't stop just because things got rough. I had to be the strength for my babies and husband. During the day, I worked as a substitute teacher while my husband was at work and my children were at school or daycare. On my lunch breaks, I would pump breast milk to store and have for my son while at daycare. I devoted my time to my family at night – helping with their schoolwork, styling my daughter's hair, and cooking a home-cooked meal every night. On church nights, I let my daughter pick a meal for us to cook out of my busy mom's cookbook. I liked it because the meals totaled ten minutes after a ten- or fifteen-minute prep time. She enjoyed it because it made her feel a part. The added touch was putting on her one of the aprons my mom made or letting her put on a plastic garbage bag to "wash the dishes" – more like play in the water.

Every night, I would take my children a bath and teach them to say *The Lord's Prayer*. My husband would make it home in time to read them a bedtime story of their choosing and a biblical story of our choosing. While they slept, I did my homework and housework. I either washed clothes, ironed them, or hung them in everyone's respected closets. My husband had a clean, starched uniform for every day of the week, and my daughter had clean, pressed uniforms for school. They both had a packed lunch with an encouraging note inside to put a smile on their face when they ate.

Before retiring for the night, I devoted time to God and sought Him for guidance. I sang uplifting songs and prayed for help to be better than I was the day before. While listening to music, I did a 15-to-30-minute exercise routine and prepared my things for the next day. This distinctive routine helped me for the years ahead as a full-time teacher in the public school system in 2006 and a full-time mommy.

NO ORDINARY TUTOR

I accepted a position as a tutor at the Job Corp in Flint. My job was to help those aspiring to obtain their G.E.D. or equivalent high school diploma in math. This was no ordinary assignment, and I was no ordinary instructor.

My boss tried to prepare me for what I had to face in dealing with the students' attitudes and behaviors—some of which were not that much younger than me. The security guards warned me of the number of fights and arguments they had to break up on a day-to-day basis. Even the students (most of which were tall young men) took dibs on how long it would take to break me. Yet, I accepted the challenge.

My first day was stressful. I left with a headache. I felt I didn't accomplish anything after 15 minutes. It was as if all my hours in college learning about classroom management and even more time as a long-term substitute teacher didn't prepare me for what I had to face in real life. At one point, I became so frustrated with the classroom's behavior that I continued lecturing louder than them stating, "I don't care. I'm gonna get paid regardless." It may have been accurate, but it was wrong to say. After I repented and asked God for help, He sent my husband to encourage me with the words: "People don't care how much you know until they know how much you care." That night, I prayed for the students and asked God to help me be a ray of hope for them. He revealed ways to help me reach those I was responsible for teaching. He said, "I didn't have you go through all those years in the military for it not to be at your advantage. Start there!"

Even though I only had a few weeks to prepare them to pass the math portion of their test, I took the time to reintroduce myself. Instead of starting with my background as a valedictorian or my degree in college, I shared with them my struggles and how hard I had to fight. I shared my military background, all the places I traveled, and my struggles in high school. I even told them about my initial fear of taking on the position, but how I was determined not to give up because they depended on me.

Saying so sparked questions and conversation. One gentleman asked, "Are you for real? You were in the Army?" He went on to ask, "You mean you did all that hardcore stuff like pushups, fighting, and using a gun?" I nodded in confirmation, but they didn't believe me. I ended the conversation by giving them all a simple wager.

"For every 15 minutes of uninterrupted teaching, I will personally give you five one-armed pushups."

One guy blurted, "IN A DRESS?" I smiled as if it were a piece of cake, nodded, and said, "In a dress!"

This was no ordinary reach, but I made one of the guys who gave me the biggest headache the timekeeper. I told him he was responsible for alerting me when my fifteen minutes were up. He would have to restart the time if anyone disrupted the class or interrupted my teaching.

The time grew close when the class started shuffling their chairs, banging on their desks, chanting, "Pushups, pushups…" I looked over to the timekeeper and said, "Sorry. I need you to restart the time." I thought the class would be angry and chaotic. Instead, they handled it like adults and eyeballed each other not to mess it up the next time.

At the 14-minute mark, I looked back at the class, placing my hand behind my ear as if to beg for some noise. This time, the class smiled and laughed quietly. They were not going to screw it up again. They wanted my one-armed pushups. When I knocked them out of the park, the class went into an uproar. They didn't need me to prove anything else to them. God had helped me reach them. From that day forward, 15 minutes of uninterrupted class time became the whole two hours of concentration, listening, dedication, and determination. They looked forward to seeing me every session and hearing something new about me every time before class began. In the end, over half received their G.E.Ds.

2 Thousand Six

f I had my way, I would have been a pediatrician or a dentist. However, I asked God to reveal what His will was for me. In a dream, I wasn't wearing a white coat with the initials MD behind my name. I wasn't standing over someone commanding them to open wide. I was dressed up in heels in front of a group of people, pointing and explaining how to solve problems. I made those listening laugh as I explained the problems. God confirmed that my field of study was in education.

God was preparing me early in life as a young girl to do His will as an instructor. This was the year He taught me how to teach.

After tutoring and subbing at a few charter schools, my first assignment was as a long-term substitute teacher in a rural environment. A fourth-grade teacher decided to retire in the middle of the school year. Besides the lunch aide and custodian, I was the only African American staff in the school. It was not an easy road to travel. I had staff and parents who challenged my expertise. When a parent who was also a teacher there wanted to pull her son from my class because she didn't' feel I was qualified to teach her gifted son, the principal stepped up for me. She said, "Mrs. Lynn was *highly* recommended for this position. If I had a son, I would want him in her class." The parent-teacher continued giving me a hard time. Weeks later, she removed her son from my classroom.

I wanted to give up, but I didn't. Like a student, if I wanted to elevate to the next level, I had to yield to my teacher – God. He was teaching me patience – something I didn't have at first. He reminded me daily to kill hate with love and treat coldness with kindness. Whenever I saw the woman or her son, I gave them the proper greeting of the day. Most times, I didn't receive a reply. When I heard that her son performed worst in the classroom of her choice, I prayed for him.

By the end of the school year, there were many layoffs. I, too, received a pink slip. Several months later, the same parent ran into me, literally. It was a cold, snowy day. I was on my way to meet my husband at his job. My children were with me when, all of a sudden, a car slid and rammed me in the rear. My car was okay, but the other car continued to slide and crashed into a pole.

The weather conditions grew worse. Finally, the driver of the other car knocked on my window and asked if I were okay. Apologetically, she gave me her information and requested mine. When I looked up, and she saw my face, she cried in disbelief. "Mrs. Lynn? Do you remember me?"

How could I forget? I smiled and replied, "Yes." She said she was hoping to me see me again under different circumstances and told me about her son's struggles. She apologized for how she treated me and explained how her way of coping was lashing out at those who cared.

I gave her my information along with a hug of forgiveness. It was one of the best feelings in the world.

NO ORDINARY APPLICATION

I put in several applications in the public school system. I kept up to date with the Michigan website for teachers. I knew when a new position was posted. I applied for a 5th-grade position that opened up. I was reluctant because it was a charter school. Though I liked the curriculum, I had my share of being overworked and underpaid, only to be let go at a moment's notice. When I interviewed for the position, I was hired on the spot. Before taking the job, I informed the administrator that I may have an upcoming interview at a different school. She thought it was my way of asking for more money. She offered me $5,000 more than the contractual salary. I gladly accepted. She showed me my classroom; only it wasn't a classroom. It was a super-large room that was used as storage. It was hot, dusty, smelly, and packed from front to rear and top to bottom with some of everything.

I got hired on a Friday evening. That Saturday was the only day I had to transform this unordinary room into a classroom, decorated and full of 5th-grade material. My mom volunteered to help me get it together. When she saw the room for the first time, her eyes grew wide in disbelief. How were we to pull this off in so little time? With gloves, bleach, Pine-Sol, cut-up t-shirts, and gospel music playing, we hopped on the challenge.

Before we knew it, the custodians were asking if we were ready to go. We had been there from 8:00 a.m. until 11:00 that night. With barking feet and aching backs, my mom and I high-fived each other. I let my mom know how much I appreciated her and that I couldn't have done it without her. She gave all the credit to God. We thanked Him and prayed for a successful school year.

On our way out, we took one last glance at our hard work. She looked at me and said something I never want to forget, "Jamillah? I'm proud of you, Girl."

It was my first full-time position as a teacher. After three weeks of long hours with no planning time or lunch break, my classroom size grew from 26 to 28 students. Then, from 28 students to 31. An increase of two to four students may not seem like much. However, with every student comes unique circumstances. They knew I was no ordinary teacher. I cared about their individual needs, families, and their futures. I wanted what was best for them. But I couldn't give them my best if I didn't have sufficient time to refuel and be at my best. I expressed my concerns to the administrative staff. They simply told me to hang in there.

I hadn't heard from the other jobs I applied for. I was convinced that the charter school was where I would spend my year. When a colleague of mine encouraged me to re-try in her school district, I didn't hesitate. At the time, her school wasn't looking for any new teachers, but the other elementary school in the district was. The two schools were like night and day. The other had a predominately White staff, including the principal, assistant principal, and secretary. The school my friend taught at was the exact opposite.

NO ORDINARY INTERVIEW

After weeks of waiting, I decided to go in person because I saw the open posting on the website. When I entered, the secretary never greeted me or acknowledged my presence. Finally, I said, "Hello." Not looking up to return the gesture, she said, "State your business." I told her that I saw the position online and was wondering if they had received it. I also shared how I wanted to leave my resume. I left there feeling down.

When I left that building, I drove over to say "hello" to my colleague and to update her on how things were going. She insisted I talk to her principal even though they weren't hiring at the moment. The instant I walked into the office, the secretary greeted me and asked how she could help me. She told me to wait a moment before meeting the principal. Minutes later, the principal came out of her office and asked why I was inquiring about a job. After explaining, she asked, "Do you mind doing an on-the-spot interview?" *Do I?*

After the interview, she wanted to see me teach a lesson. I thought she wanted to hear how I would teach in a typical scenario. No, she walked me down to one of the 2nd-grade classrooms in her building. Before entering, she warned how they were a rowdy group with new faces. She added more pressure by stating, "If you can manage to pull off a lesson with this group, you belong in this school."

What kind of lesson could I do that would be fun to teach while engaging the class and keeping their undivided attention? After praying, God gave me to teach punctuation using a dry erase board with colored dry erase markers. As I held up three markers, I told the students that a yellow marker meant to pause or slow down, a red marker meant to stop, and a green marker meant to keep going.

We did a trial run. Then, I had volunteers come up to the board. The 2nd-grade teacher, the students, and the principal were pleased with my presentation. After I finished, the principal expressed the possibility of forming another 3rd-grade class but could not guarantee it. She said she would keep in touch.

That night, I received the call that the job was mine if I wanted it. I gladly accepted. She told me that some people call her the principal who hires "Black folks." She said, "In case you're wondering, I did my homework. I called all of your references. Should you hear that rumor, just know I didn't hire you because you are Black. I hired you because you came highly qualified."

NO ORDINARY CLASSROOM

Like before, I had less than two days to get my classroom together and learn the curriculum. All of the classrooms were occupied. The only room available was used as a conference room. The good news was that I didn't have to clear out a lot of things. The bad news was that the school's budget was low, and funding didn't allow space for me to fill the classroom. I had to pull items from several places to create a unique environment for children to learn. It was as if I were given a blank canvas without the tools to draw. Teachers sporadically offered me their unwanted wall art, stationery supplies, or books. It gave me something to work with. Another teacher (who remained a source of strength and guidance) introduced me to what the school called "The Chicken Coop."

The Chicken Coop was an oversized storage room with any and everything in it. You could find whatever you needed to find if you had the time, patience, and manpower to sift through the piles. It was true: "Someone else's trash was my treasure." In that short period of time, I befriended the custodian, a couple of teachers, and even the secretary. Together, we transformed a once dull, empty space into a warm, welcoming environment. I had a like-new teacher's desk with a rolling chair. Another teacher gifted me a nice area rug for circle time, and the principal gave me a heavy-duty pencil sharpener as a welcoming gift. The only thing left for me to do was apply my knowledge and experience to help transform the lives of eighteen 3rd-grade students.

NO ORDINARY FLIP

My 3rd-grade classroom was known as "The Underdogs." Our initial reading level was below 2nd grade. Our math testing average was below 50%. I had very little time to turn things around for them/us. I did the only thing I knew to do – I prayed. I did so every day at home on my knees, at school by touching their lockers and desks, and while teaching or handing out assignments.

My motto was that school should always be fundamental, with an emphasis on the word fun. God constantly fed me with fun and innovative ideas to keep them engaged.

As time passed, my classroom average performance increased to 56% and then to 68%. God revealed to me that He had done what I did in setting up my classroom – turned nothing into something.

2 Thousand Seven

NO ORDINARY EDUCATOR

"Give instruction to a wise man, and he will be still wiser; teach a righteous man, and he will increase in learning."

— [PROVERBS 9:9] —

The first year of teaching 3rd-grade was a wonderful experience. I had familiarized myself with the curriculum, started to feel comfortable partnering with my coworkers, and adapted to the expectations of my principal. I was snug right where I was. I soon realized that my comfort zone was not a place for God. He had no room to move there.

When Edriece and I received news that we were expecting another son, I experienced more complications. Since I had two miscarriages before this pregnancy, I was put on strict bed rest for a couple of weeks as a precautionary measure. I didn't want to inform my principal, especially after all she had done to hire me. But she said, "Lynn, this school is going to be here whether you are or not. This school is going to stand whether you fall. Take care of yourself and that baby you're carrying."

Weeks of bed rest eventually turned into a couple of months. Those months resulted in the early arrival of my youngest son. Since he arrived at the start of the new school year, my new students had several substitutes. When I returned from maternity leave, things were not as I had hoped.

This was the year God showed me how NOT to limit myself but to exercise the gift He had birthed in me.

NO ORDINARY GRADE

Although I had returned to teach the same grade, I didn't have the same classroom. Not only that, I had a new principal, complete with a new school building and a brand-new name. What once were two small separate elementary schools was now one large school under new leadership. The principal I had grown to love declined the position as an assistant principal under the administration of the other principal who had less time and seniority. Given the circumstances, it would have been a slap in the face.

With the new school came new faces and a new set of rules. The students no longer sat quietly in the morning to read books or go over homework. They now got to play in the gym for periods, which caused them to come to class wired and full of energy. It was challenging to wind them down and prepare for the day's assignments. Still, I continued to use my previous way of doing things to incorporate fun with learning. The difference was that some of my classroom management consisted of strict routines. The students grew to love it, but the principal not so much. She called my methods unorthodox and my style too militant. I could no longer line students in the hallway and drill them on math facts or the previous night's homework assignments before entering my classroom. The famous "I'll wait" teacher stare was forbidden to discourage students from leaning back in their chairs or to encourage them to sit up straight with both feet on the floor.

I had to change and modify my way of doing things, especially after receiving an overall unsatisfactory on my teacher evaluation. I was shocked, not because I was some great wonder who had already reached her full potential. I knew there was room for growth being a new hire. But an overall unsatisfactory? I would have accepted areas of "need improvement" better. It was insulting. To top it off, this was the same principal who rejected my application. She was as cold as the day I first entered her building. Who was she to give me an unsatisfactory?

I became angry. I made up in my mind that I wasn't going to smile at her or any of the teachers she socialized with. I figured they had formulated opinions about me anyway. Then God, through my mother, gave me sound advice. She asked, "So what? What if they don't like you? They didn't like Jesus!" She reminded me that it wasn't about me but the children. And she was right. I repented and asked God to help me be what He needed me to be—a light.

It wasn't long before I modified my approach to teaching without compromising my style. The saying "When in Rome do as the Romans do" doesn't mean to become weak and forget who you are. I believe it means something greater – to yield, to be understanding, and to learn how to work harmoniously together if possible. I learned my new principal and respected what she wanted for our school. As a result, I soon earned the respect of her leadership and my coworkers. In times of friction with parents, it was this same principal who stood up for me.

NO ORDINARY OBSESSION

I watched the movie *Sleeping with the Enemy*. In it, the actress Julia Roberts played the wife of a man with OCD. Among other things, he had to have his canned goods facing a certain way on the right shelf in his cabinet. The hand towels in his bathroom had to be a certain width and length while being evenly spaced on the rack. I disliked how he treated his wife, but I remember thinking, *"I really like how organized he is."* It gave me a sense of relief to see things in order. Although I may have had a slight touch of OCD before being in the military, I am certain Uncle Sam aided in my obsession. I found pleasure in having my wardrobe hung on the same type of hanger, a certain distance apart, having my socks and underwear rolled a particular way, or having my shoes facing the same direction. It carried over into my home life and, ultimately, work life.

At home, my husband's work uniforms were always washed, folded, ironed, and hung facing a certain way. The only thing he had to do was choose whether he was wearing long or short sleeves. His dress suits were color-coordinated and facing the same direction on suit hangers. It was the same for each of my children. Whenever I had to go out of town, it was easy for my husband or babysitters to pick out my children's attire or find something in the cabinets to cook.

I don't believe they cared half as much as I did. Still, I took pride in doing it because it gave me a feeling of satisfaction.

I can see how someone might confuse someone like me as a perfectionist. However, OCD can be a debilitating condition impacting work, relationships, or even school. It's far more drastic than someone wanting a flawless result in a task. I would describe it as an irresistible urge to do things to relieve stress and feel better. Ignoring these urges while having this condition was not easy because the desires would come back again later. It was only by the grace of God that I managed to keep it under wraps.

2 Thousand Eight

NO ORDINARY HOUSE

*"Through wisdom is an house builded; and
by understanding it is established."*

[PROVERBS 24:3]

After entering the second full year of teaching, my husband and I learned that we were increasing our family size by two feet. It called for a bigger vehicle and a larger house. We had already done what most growing families did and purchased a minivan. Shortly after, my husband was in a rollover accident that totaled the minivan. Since we purchased gap insurance on it, we were able to buy a new van. Now, it was time to move on out and move on up.

We were faced with two major choices: Will we be able to sell our current home? If we had to rent it, who would we rent it to? This was the year God blessed us with a better home in a nicer neighborhood.

We took our time searching for the perfect house that fit our needs. We learned from our first experience not to rush the process but to be patient and to choose a realtor that had our best interest at heart. We did just that.

After viewing several homes, we narrowed our decision to a home that best fit our budget. It didn't necessarily have the "it" factor, but I knew we could possibly grow to love it. When my husband sensed that I was going to settle, he asked our realtor if we could look at one more house. It was one outside of our price range. We only considered it as a possibility if my husband had gotten hired at a job he desired at the MTA (Mass Transportation Authority). When we didn't receive word, we pushed the thought aside.

When our realtor set up the showing, I was so excited. My husband remained reserved. He reminded me like he did before we entered each home on our list, "Don't smile and don't show your hand!" I knew it would be hard to do, especially if I really liked the house, but I agreed.

NO ORDINARY DECISION

The realtor was awaiting our arrival. I loved the neighborhood and the fact it was located directly across from an elementary school with a nice park. I said, "Ooh, Honey, the children can walk to school." They attended the same school I taught at a year after I hired in, so that was something they had never experienced since we lived miles away.

My husband always wanted a deck. This house had two—one outside the enormous family room and another outside the upstairs bedroom. I always wanted a walk-in closet and a bathroom in the master bedroom. This house had both. My husband and I wanted our daughter, Imari, to have a bedroom that matched the size of her creative imagination. This house had a bedroom waiting just for her. My oldest son, Edriece, Jr., loved books, so I jokingly mentioned, "It would be nice if he had a room with a built-in bookshelf." This house did. It was everything we wanted, plus some added features: a utility room, a library/study, a mud room, a skylight, and plenty of cabinets and storage space. That's a teacher's dream! And as if the garage and finished basement weren't enough, it had central air. It may not have meant much to someone else, but I had my share of sleeping in the heat.

This was definitely no ordinary house. To start, each bedroom and bathroom door had clear, crystal doorknobs. In the front of the house were huge evergreen bushes in front of a huge bay window. Surrounding the house were several windows in all the other rooms, causing the natural light to bring out its beauty. Each room had a unique wall texture. The guest room had an all-black texture. The library had built-in shelving covering pegged walls and a window overseeing the mud room. The children's bathroom had fairly odd wallpaper that made it exquisite. The walls leading down to the basement reminded me of being in a cave. They were brown with a stone feel. I can't forget about the kitchen. Before that day, I had never seen or even heard of a kitchen with metal cabinets; even more so, the cabinets each had round, clear knobs with various seeds inside. The master bathroom wasn't too out of the ordinary, but the heat lamp in the ceiling sparked my husband's interest. The guest bathroom was probably the most distinctive with its silver psychedelic wallpaper on all walls, including the window shade, ceiling, plug covers, light switch, and door.

We were about to leave when I smelled a foul smell coming from my six-month-old son's diaper. The realtor joked and said, "I guess he's making his mark on the house." I asked to change his diaper before we left. The realtor gave a worried look as if I were planning to dispose of it inside somewhere. She was relieved when she saw me pull a disposable baggie from his diaper bag.

I had made up my mind that this house had the "it" factor. I even tried to convince my husband by telling him that he could make the finished basement his man cave, but there was no need. He received his sign from God as we walked towards our car. I was busy looking at the possibility of planting flowers when my husband got my attention and said, "Bae! Come here. You ain't gone believe this!" I assumed it was something horrible, like some electrical wiring needing to be replaced. When he pulled me close and said, "Look down," I knew otherwise. There, engraved in the driveway, was the name "Eric," spelled exactly like that of our baby son.

NO ORDINARY OFFER

It wasn't long before he called the realtor and stated, "We're ready to make an offer." We hadn't decided on the amount just yet. Days later, my husband said that we would pray about it and call her with a number. I asked God to do like He did with Gideon in the Bible as it pertained to the fleece and dew. I wanted to be sure and very sure it was His will. So, I told myself that however many calories I burned on the treadmill that morning, I would tack on the word "thousand" at the end of it. I usually burned around 100 to

115 in the 15 minutes I set aside before showering and going to work. That morning, I was running behind and only ran for ten minutes. When I looked at the calories burned, I said, "We can't offer that amount. Nevertheless, Lord, I made a vow to you."

That afternoon, after getting off work, I called my husband and told him the suggested amount and how I came up with such an unordinary figure. He laughed and exclaimed, "NO WAY!" He wanted to surprise me by putting in the offer earlier. The amount he offered her was an exact amount to the suggested offer I came up with. We both praised God in advance.

NO ORDINARY DEBT

The saying, "when it rains, it pours," is so true. The week before we closed on the new house, my husband lost his job and was desperately waiting to hear from the job he desired, or any job for that matter. He didn't want the weight of our financial obligations to fall upon my shoulders. It wasn't too bad at first. We had a little cushion. The only thing left for us to do was sell or rent our current home. After listing it for three months, we decided to rent it out. We wanted tenants as soon as possible to avoid paying two mortgage notes. That's the primary reason we ignored all the red flags when we decided to rent to a family. Soon, financial struggles forced them to move out without giving us notice. We were forced to pay two house notes for nearly a year. After months of struggling to do this, we were led to filing for bankruptcy.

This was something I never wanted to do. I had worked hard to earn and maintain a good credit score, only to have it thrown away. I became angry. I was bitter towards the family we rented to. I was furious that my husband was still out of work. Then, it was as if God whispered in my ear and asked, "What are you so upset for? Don't you know that nothing happens in life without my approval?" I swallowed my pride and realized that our situation was only a setup for a comeback.

NO ORDINARY PRAYING WOMAN

My husband always teased me by saying I had a special relationship with God. Whenever I would fast and pray or even pray at the drop of a hat, God would hear my cry and answer my prayer, giving me the desires of my heart.

There was a time when Edriece went through a season of night tremors. He would often awaken, not knowing he had caused harm to me while doing them. I anointed him with oil and prayed that God would deliver him from them. I went on to say that if there were any underlying issues, they be addressed. It wasn't a week before God had taken them away.

I also remember a time Edriece was doing yardwork before an expected heavy rain. Minutes into mowing the lawn, the lawnmower stopped working. He was quite upset. Before praying, I told him that everything would work out alright. He gave me a look of *"Okay, Woman. I don't have time for false hope right now."* I went inside and prayed. Within minutes, God started the lawnmower and allowed my husband time to finish the front and back yard. Shortly after, the lawnmower conked out, and it began raining.

That's why I decided to accept what God was saying to me about our financial struggle and those who initiated it. Soon, my heart empathized with the family who vacated our first home. I began praying for them and their finances. When I heard things were better for them, I smiled. Next, I started praying for my husband that God's will would be done. It wasn't long before my husband received a call for an interview at the very job he so desired.

It was tradition to ask the pastor for prayer before any major surgery, purchase, or move. So, my husband asked our pastor to pray over his application. When he did, he gave my husband instructions to pack a sack lunch for the interview. He said, "If they ask you, 'What's in the bag?' You tell them it's your lunch just in case they need you to start immediately."

His interview was early the next morning. He was running behind and didn't get a chance to pack the sack lunch. When he opened the refrigerator to grab a quick bite to eat, he saw that I had already prepared it with a note that said, "Here's your lunch, Honey. You got this. I love you."

Days later, he received a letter of denial. Shortly afterward, he received a call from the company telling him to disregard the letter and congratulating him as a new hire.

God constantly showed us that we can always look to Him for anything. Before long, my credit score, which had plummeted after the bankruptcy, had risen back to good credit standing.

NO ORDINARY NEIGHBORS

In our former home, we were blessed to have such friendly neighbors. In fact, leaving them was a tough decision. My husband would carpool with the husband to work while the wife would give me garden tips or help with my little ones. They were awesome. We felt we wouldn't find another couple so kind, generous, and trusting… until we did.

Usually, neighbors ask to borrow things like butter, sugar, or even eggs. In our case, we were quite the bunch. On the day we moved most of our boxes and furniture into the house, we didn't think about the water not being turned on yet. When one of our children asked to use the bathroom, we assumed it would be in the form of water. Instead, it was the solid form. We couldn't allow that horrible smell to sit overnight. It had already stunk up the entire house. So, we walked next door, introduced ourselves, and asked to borrow a bucket of water. After hearing the story behind our dire need, our new neighbors laughed. Over the course of time, we have become more like family. In time, their questions and doubts regarding faith were strengthened.

2 Thousand Fourteen

When it's time to leave the nest, a mother bird makes everything quite uncomfortable for her baby birds. Painful as it was, God revealed that it was time for my family and I to flap our wings and fly to launch our own ministry. Shortly before this time, the enemy tried to ruin long-running friendships, my marriage, and even my career, but God blocked it. It was a wake-up call for me not to take things and people for granted. This was the year He showed me that ministry isn't just about a building's physical location but about the actual process of construction. It required redeveloping friendships, endurance, and strength.

NO ORDINARY SERVANTS

Before marrying Edriece, I was active in my local church and community. I volunteered after school as a tutor, helped during city efforts, and volunteered in the summer as a Vacation Bible School teacher. He, too, did various things both inside and outside ministry. When we married, we worked together doing whatever our hands found to do. It was never for attention or recognition but always as an act of selfless service.

Certain circumstances pushed us out of the nest. My husband had already served ten years before I joined his church. Together, we faithfully served ten more years before moving our membership.

As excited as I was for my husband and the other ministers ordained as elders, I wasn't ready to leave behind my extended family to put in the work required to start a new ministry. That's why it came as quite a surprise when the pastor announced over the floor that he gave his blessings to anyone (referring to the newly ordained elders) who was ready to launch their ministry. I couldn't blame my husband for his enthusiasm. After all, he had served faithfully for twenty years with an additional three. It was time. Ready or not, we had to go.

NO ORDINARY CHURCH

Edriece shared with me how he'd seen a church for rent. "The location is perfect," he exclaimed! It was. It was in the heart of the city—not too far from our home or jobs. I felt the rent was outside our budget and that the landlord was overcharging us for the amount of work needed to get the place up to code. Nonetheless, I wanted to support my husband. He deserved it. I focused on the church's potential.

It was no ordinary building. I believe it used to be an old car dealership. The tan, all-brick building standing on a corner lot needed tons of work. God trusted us to put in the leg work in beautifying His house.

The former pastor had passed away and left the church to his son. Being a truck driver, the son decided to rent the church out to a couple of people before us. When they left, the place had gone unkept for some time. It was more work than my husband and I could take on by ourselves. Yet, I remained hopeful. Every day before starting any project, I would pray and ask God to send on help. I asked Him to send couples, young people, willing workers, and souls hungry and thirsty for righteousness.

Since school was out during the summer, my children worked alongside me every day. My husband always joined us at the end of the day when he got off work to do necessary things like plumbing. My sister and her two youngest children would help put in work too. We did everything from pulling weeds to removing the rubbish on the outside and painting to clearing out space on the inside.

A man came by and asked if he could offer some help. He told us that he worked at a nearby high school. After my husband and I accepted his offer, he returned with flowers and plants. The next day, he returned with two more men who helped us finish painting the outside, giving it a fresh, new look. It was motivating to witness the hand of God.

After the sanctuary was complete, my family and I began having prayer service. As I attempted to play the keyboard, my 12-year-old daughter would sing while my eight-year-old and five-year-old sons alternated taking turns on the bongos and drums. My husband would end with encouraging words followed by prayer. Visitors became members, and soon, we had a growing church family. We hung up our sign with the name of our church and hours of operation. We were ready to have our grand opening and serve in the community.

NO ORDINARY TEAM

It's true; there's no "I" in "team." Since my husband worked the second shift, I thought I had to carry the load of ministry. Instead of allowing more time to pass by or waiting for God to send on more souls to the ministry, I did what I could to be a helpmate for my husband. I would leave work, go home, prepare dinner, and turn around, making several trips to pick up anyone who needed a ride to church. Even when I decided to trade in my brand-new SUV for a larger vehicle to minimize the number of trips, it still wasn't enough to offset all the things we had going on.

One would think my husband and I would be frustrated, but we were no ordinary team. We kept a positive attitude and did our level best to provide a warm and welcoming atmosphere. We put on big programs and sold dinners to help offset ministry costs. A couple of months had passed. Still, my husband was concerned about everything I had taken on, especially while continuing to teach and mother our children. I assured him that I was fine, until I wasn't.

2 Thousand Fifteen

NO ORDINARY FALL

"For a righteous man may fall seven times and rise again..."

— [PROVERBS 24:16A] —

---

alls are categorized into two basic types: elevated or same-level. Slips and trips are the most common same-level falls. The more severe type is elevated falls. In either case, falling is never easy. If others witness it, you may be embarrassed. If you're alone, you may need help after a hard one. For me, falling was never fun. Prior to this year, I had fallen down a flight of stairs, slipped and fell on some ice face-forward while pregnant, and tripped over something in the road while running the ten-mile Crim. I was on my seventh mile when I fell during the run. To turn around and walk (more like limp) back would have taken longer than just finishing the last three miles.

Falling itself is inevitable. I believe everyone at one point in life has experienced a fall, whether as a child or an adult.

Toddlers may cry a little, but they know Mommy or Daddy will help them get back up. The child doesn't dwell on the fall but smiles in appreciation for being helped up. Why can't we do this as adults? We cry more instead of reaching out to our "Father." We think that asking for help is a form of weakness. We dwell on the fact that we fell instead of what happens after the fall.

At the start of the school year, I had something fall on me at work. It was my last class for the day, so I had changed out of some fashionable shoes into some soft, comfy ones. They were the kind a woman could fold and place into her purse to switch into if wearing heels became unbearable. They were probably the flattest flats I owned, but somehow my feet felt good in them. I don't even think they had soles on them. They almost felt like thin socks. That's why it hurt like heck when a desk fell right on my foot after answering a student's question.

The fall itself was quick and easy. The pain after the fall was the hard part. Students gathered around in shock instead of getting the table off my foot. It was one of those old-fashioned tables with two metal drawers, making it extremely heavy. When I yelled "HELP" repeatedly, it got their attention. The two students who sat at the desk underestimated its weight. When they tried to lift it, the desk slipped out of their hands and right back onto my foot, crushing my big toe and spraining two other toes. That's when I felt every ounce of pain a person could feel. I remember waking up in the middle of the night in agony, telling my husband that the pain was worse than labor.

I took the necessary time to heal. Then, I returned to work with a boot and crutches. I didn't quit.

This was the year God showed me that my falling was not my failure. God revealed His strength in my willingness to get back up again. He confirmed that by putting my trust in Him and holding on to His unchanging hand was my plan in getting up. He didn't want me to look to others, not doctors, lawyers, family, or friends. He didn't want me to rely on things like the government or disability benefits as a hand*out*. He wanted me to rely solely on Him for a hand *up*.

Everything that seemed to fall apart this year gave me more reason to trust God and believe Him to put me back together again.

NO ORDINARY STOP

My three children and my two nieces came with me to visit my father in Pennsylvania. While there, he introduced us to his wife and showed us around. The next day, we went out to dinner. I had already warned them about my father's Islamic beliefs and told them not to order anything with pork in it. So, they didn't. However, it didn't stop my father's interrogations leading into the "gray areas" of our lives.

"So, Tashara, what are some things you like to order on your pizza?" he asked.

"I like cheese and pepperoni on mine, Grandpa," she said.

"Um, hmmph. You don't say? What about you, Imari? What do you like on your pizza?"

"I like cheese and ham, Grandpa!" she exclaimed.

"Me too," my oldest son, EJ, added.

Sensing where the conversation was heading, his wife said, "Not now, Jamal. Just leave them alone."

The conversation turned into a heated discussion. Why couldn't he just take her advice? I had hoped this trip would be the start of rekindling our relationship. Instead, he ruined it by focusing on a subject that didn't matter more than the fact we drove hundreds of miles to visit him.

He yelled, "I AIN'T PAYING FOR NO GRANDCHILDREN OF MINE TO BE EATING PORK!"

He made a huge scene. I made an even bigger one. I ignored the voice of God telling me to hush. In place, I blurted out, "YOU DON'T HAVE TO PAY JACK! I GOT MY OWN MONEY!" I don't know what it is about the use of improper English during an argument, but it was gratifying. Deep down inside, I wanted to cry. Even at the age of forty, I wanted my father to be my dad. I was willing to ignore and bypass all the wrong he had done to my mom, sister, and me. I was willing to overlook and accept the apology I would never receive. But pride got in the way. Just like the scripture, warning came before my destruction, and my pride came before a fall.

"Y'ALL, LET'S GO!" I yelled as I grabbed my purse.

My nieces and children looked so confused. They didn't want to leave their grandfather. They were enjoying his funny stories and distinct laugh. Yet, I couldn't do it anymore. It was time to go, and I was willing to cut my trip short.

I wanted to speed off and leave, but I couldn't. I had no clue how to get to where I was going, even with the Garmin GPS my father had gifted me the day I arrived. That's why I was so happy when his wife followed me to the car. She insisted I calm down and stay the night. When I declined, she offered to at least ride with me long enough to show me where to get on the expressway. My father followed close behind.

Not long after I left the restaurant, I apparently ran a blinking yellow light. I learned later that Wall, Pennsylvania was *not* a good place for me to get pulled over, especially at night. Not long after I was pulled over, the police officer approached my window and asked for my license and registration. When I handed it to him, he yanked it and walked back to his vehicle before I could ask why he pulled me over. I sat in my car, waiting patiently for him to return. My children and nieces were scared out of their wits. My oldest asked, "Mommy, are you going to jail?" When she said that, my youngest son burst into tears.

NO ORDINARY WALL

What in the world was taking so long? By now, I had become impatient. When two other police cars surrounded me, I grew frustrated. The adrenaline from the restaurant incident was already pumping when I said, "REALLY? IT TAKES THREE POLICE CARS TO PULL ME OVER?" The glare from all the flashing lights gave me an instant headache, causing most of my agitation. Marjorie insisted I stay calm and wait for the first officer to inform me why I was stopped in the first place. After waiting what seemed to be fifteen more minutes, I became antsy. Shortly after, a fourth police car surrounded me. If I wanted to, I couldn't escape. They had me walled in. Maybe that's why they call it *Wall, Pennsylvania*.

Before I knew it, something came over me. It was as if I had a flashback of being overseas in Kuwait. I was furious.

I said, "That did it!" Then, without thinking, I jumped out of the car and yelled, "WHAT THE HECK?" Instantly, every police officer was armed and ready with guns drawn and demanding that I get back into my car.

"No!" I said, insisting someone tell me why was I being pulled over.

"MA'AM, WE'RE NOT GONNA TELL YOU AGAIN! GET YOUR A#% BACK INTO YOUR CAR!"

I became the female version of "The Hulk" at this point.

"ARE YOU GONNA SHOOT ME IN FRONT OF MY CHILDREN? HUH?"

The officer who pulled me over grabbed my arm and slammed me face forward against my car, handcuffing me.

"GREAT! FOUR POLICE CARS? FOUR? FOR A BLINKING YELLOW LIGHT?"

The officer yanked me and started reading me my rights. My resistance caused my top to pull down, nearly exposing myself. With tears rolling down my face, I asked, "WHERE WERE YOU WHEN I GOT MOLESTED? HUH? WHERE WERE YOU WHEN I GOT RAPED? NOWHERE!"

My dad asked if he could get out of his vehicle. They allowed him to say a few words to me before taking me to jail. He explained how I had never been in any trouble with the law and how I had served my country well. It didn't matter. I was now placed in the back of a police car headed to their county jail.

When I arrived, the arresting police officer appeared to have pity.

"Why didn't you just get back into your car?" he asked, shaking his head. "You're lucky we don't charge you with disorderly conduct."

Instead of responding, I sniffed my snot, fought back the tears, and pretended to be tough by shrugging my shoulders.

When I came to myself, I couldn't believe what had happened. Who was that person? It was out of the norm for me. I had camouflaged my emotions too long, and things were eating me up from the inside out that I thought I had buried. I somehow managed to simmer my feelings for years, but this seemed to be the incident that triggered it all. Thankfully, it was not something that was on my record. As a teacher, I couldn't afford to let this be my downfall. It did, however, prompt me to seek help from a therapist.

NO ORDINARY TRAUMA

Over the course of the years, my family doctor became more like a father to my family and me. When he decided to retire, I cried as if he had passed away. I was happy for him to enjoy his life after faithfully servicing the community for over forty years. Before retiring, he recommended me to a mental therapist, particularly after my recent outburst with the law. He believed it may have revived my suppressed feelings, calling it PTSD or Post Traumatic Stress Disorder. My first thought was, *"Black people don't see shrinks."* My second thought was, *"People who trust and believe in God don't see crazy doctors."*

He must've read my thoughts because he insisted I give group therapy a try. So, I did. I didn't like it at all. I found myself empathizing and sympathizing with everyone else. When it was time to hear my issues, I felt they weren't extreme enough to share. When I requested a one-on-one, it was with an older guy with whom I didn't seem to connect. Not wanting to base everything on my initial visit with him, I tried a second time. But, when he seemed to brush everything off as if it were nothing, even after pouring my heart out on my second visit, I wanted to stop going. I felt no empathy or ounce of compassion. Then, my family doctor asked me how the therapy sessions were going. After telling him, I thought he would give me an "A" for effort, but he urged me to try again with someone else. I am so happy I took his advice. My therapist was nothing like I imagined but everything I needed. With her help and guidance, I was able to deal with the stress associated with past and recent events, anxiety, and my impulsive and compulsive acts. She worked together with a psychologist to help get me back on track. They helped kill my thoughts about seeing a mental therapist by asking me two questions: "Do you go to the doctor when you're feeling sick? Do you take the medication they prescribe to help you feel better? It's the same thing here; only it's not for your body; it's for your mind."

NO ORDINARY PLUMMET

As I approached the months leading up to receiving my tenure, my migraines increased in intensity and frequency. To make matters worst, it dawned on me that I had been shifted nearly every year. It was to be expected, especially since I hadn't made tenure. Still, most teachers got to keep their same classroom. Moving from one classroom to the next required a lot of work. In my case, it was triple the work. I had to have order, neatness, and cleanliness.

I went from teaching 3rd grade to 4th grade, 4th grade to 6th grade, and 6th grade to teaching gym. Then, I went from teaching gym to kindergarten and kindergarten to art. At first, I felt humiliated. Maybe I was more insulted than anything. After all, I didn't go through years of obtaining my bachelor's and master's degrees to teach gym or art. I believed that no other teacher had been shuffled around as much as I. Still, no matter where I was placed, I vowed to do my best and give my all. My problem was that I had no off button.

I should've learned my lesson the year I taught physical education. As I assembled a classroom of kindergartners, I felt the entire gymnasium spinning. I shook it off at first and continued instructing the students how to play the game *Duck Duck Goose*. Then, I thought, in the words of Nelly, *"It's getting hot in here!"* So, I went to get a drink of water in the hallway. Before I could press the button, I passed out and hit the floor. The school secretary must have seen me on the cameras because, when I came to, my head was in the principal's lap.

"Jamillah? Are you okay?" she asked.

"I think so," I said as I rubbed the knot on the back of my head. "My ponytail must've cushioned the fall."

We laughed as the ambulance put me on the gurney. "Thank goodness for your pony!"

The spinning and dizziness continued for days. I described it as being on a merry-go-round and a roller coaster at the same time. I had taken a week off of work while the results came back. It was found by an ear, nose, and throat doctor or ENT that I had labyrinthitis, which later caused vertigo. The anxiety associated with these unusual episodes triggered me to have chronic migraines. The migraines were intensified by stress.

Things were not looking up for me. But, instead of taking the time to rest and recover, I was determined to press my way forward. I was neck-to-neck in a race against the Energizer Bunny. It wasn't like I were due to receive a reward unless there was one given for burnout. Thankfully, God intervened. It was as if He said, "I guess I'm gonna have to sit you down myself." Shortly after that, I fell down… literally.

I was hanging up students' artwork on a cart in the hallway at school. I felt dizzy at first, but then a sharp pain pierced my temples. It was similar to someone stabbing me with a knife in the temples, head, and eyes. Then, I hit the floor.

NO ORDINARY COCKTAIL

I was rushed to the hospital. When asked to rate my pain level, I gave it a 13 on the Richter Scale. After getting evaluated, I was given a migraine cocktail. It was a mixture of medications to help lessen the severity of my migraine. Not long after the medication was in my system, I sat up and looked at my husband, who was there praying for me.

"WHAT'S WRONG, BABY?" he asked.

"I don't know. Something doesn't feel right."

Something wasn't right indeed. I became extremely hot, I broke into a sweat, my heart was racing, and my head was pounding like never before. I started to panic. When I kicked off the blanket one of the nurses had given me and practically stripped out of my hospital gown, my husband called out for a nurse. Edriece described me as looking deranged. The nurse came in, took one look at me, and hurried back with the doctor. Before he could ask any questions, I started convulsing. Before I knew it, I was having (what they called) a non-epileptic seizure. I remember being scared and confused because something like this had never happened before.

NO ORDINARY WILL

Whenever I had an episode, I would vomit and lose control of my bowels. I had to carry a cup around to puke in along with bags to minimize foul smells.

Pastor friends of my husband reached out to their neurologist. My step-mother reached out to my brother, who is a neurologist. At one point, she drove me to one of Michigan's best hospitals for answers. They stopped at nothing. I was there for days while they ran more tests, cat scans and monitored me while I slept. On the fifth day, they regretted sending me home.

I was prescribed various pills to treat the migraines. The side effects of the medicine triggered more seizures. The medicine to treat the seizures caused headaches. The medicine to treat nausea and vomiting caused dizziness. The prescription for that caused vomiting and insomnia. I needed rest to heal, but I stayed awake in pain. It was nerve-wracking!

For safety reasons, I couldn't drive. It was a "catch twenty-two" because riding with others made me dizzy and nauseous. The anxiety associated with wondering whether or not it would happen again caused it to happen... again! It was frustrating. Everyone had questions. I wanted answers that none of my local doctors had the answers to. Though my neurologist worked with a team of doctors (an ENT, gastroenterologist, and primary care physician), they failed to find the root of my condition. They only prescribed more medication in hopes that something would work.

Like David in the Bible did when he fought Goliath, I reminded myself, "If God brought me to it, surely He would bring me through it." I repeated it nearly every day until I believed it. There were days family and friends came over to see me and left in tears. On other days, people would come to pray for me, and God gave me the strength to pray for them instead. From the outside in, it looked hopeless. I was yet having the seizures, at home, at church when I went for prayer, in the car on the way to doctor visits, and sometimes while waiting to be seen at the appointment.

We apparently made too much money to qualify for government assistance but not enough to prevent the bills from piling up. I fought and fought to get approved for short-term disability through my job. When it was approved, I fought even harder for long-term disability.

My husband and mother took turns caring for my children and me. Many nights, my husband would get off of work just to watch me sleep. When he could no longer keep his eyes open, he asked his mother to sit with me. On her way to stay with me, she fell and sprained her ankle. That's when I cried to God for mercy. My will was to be healed. My will was to have a pause in everything that happened to me. As always, He reminded me that *His* will was for me to keep trusting and to be a living witness of His healing power. After I prayed, I surrendered, "Lord, not *my* will but let *Your* will be done in my life."

2 Thousand Eighteen

Whether it was a sudden change in the lease agreement or building issues, we had moved our church location four times by now. We received ridicule from outsiders. "Y'all moving again?" they would ask. They never knew the complete story. I felt deep down that Edriece was bothered by the constant changes. Whenever we moved, we gained members that we invested in and lost members along the way. If we ever needed a reason to give up, now was the time. But God showed us that, while we were moving, He was moving in us and through us. We were always in the right place at the right time. Souls were touched, and lives were changed. The moves were necessary if we were to be a spiritual airport.

This was the year God told us that our renting days were expiring. He anointed us for ownership by making our next move our best move.

NO ORDINARY REQUEST

Edriece asked me to go on a consecration fast with him at the beginning of the year. Shortly after, he asked the church to do the same. Our area of focus was on trusting God to do the unthinkable. I'm sure he meant something milder than my interpretation, but I was in too deep. I rearranged my prayer closet. I started praying more frequently and intensely for specific things like a handicap ramp. Edriece had only two desires: an actual church building, not one that someone turned into a church, and an actual landmark in the city.

When we searched together, we saw a few that were not to our liking. While he slept, I searched one more time, and only one property popped up. It appeared to be everything we asked for! The thing that stood out was its ocean blue entry doorsteps. I had never seen anything like that before, especially for a church. After seeing them, I yelled as softly as possible, "THIS IS IT!" God had the building waiting just for us.

The next morning, I showed my husband. He hid his excitement as he did when we purchased our second home. When he gave me the okay, I contacted our realtor. It had been ten years since we'd last seen her, so she was delighted to hear from us. She researched how long the building had been on the market and found out the various purchase options. That same day, she set up a showing.

Before arriving, I prayed and thanked God in advance for His grace and mercy. I said, "Lord, if You don't do anything else, You have done enough. If it is Your will, I will know when I see a handicap ramp."

When we purchased our home years ago, our realtor knew what we desired even before seeing the inside. When I shared that we hoped for a handicap ramp, she wished for one too. When we pulled into the parking lot and saw that it did, I honked the horn in praise. Our realtor smiled.

NO ORDINARY VISION

The church was even more than we had envisioned. There was no question about where we would start. Without saying a word, my husband and I held hands and opened the wooden doors leading into the sanctuary. I can't remember if the power was on in the building, but the sunlight shining through the stained-glass windows reminded me that serving the Lord does pay off after a while.

NO ORDINARY AGREEMENT

"Yes, write up the agreement," Edriece told our realtor. We didn't want to drag our feet on it. They were asking for an amount slightly higher than our budget. We made an offer that didn't put a financial burden on our members or one that rested on our shoulders. It was only a matter of time before we needed to vacate our current location. We saved enough funds to put down in the event God opened a door for us.

NO ORDINARY DOWN PAYMENT

Neither Edriece nor I realized the differences between purchasing a commercial building and a residential home. We needed 15% more than what we had. We still asked our realtor to go forward with the proposal. We bowed out gracefully when the seller submitted a counteroffer that resembled the initial offer. I knew that God was either saying "No" or "Not now," and I was not going to bargain with Him.

We didn't stress because our realtor assured us that our offer was good for a month. Additionally, we still had six to eight more months in our current building… at least we thought. After two months, we received a message that we needed to be out of our storefront in thirty days or less because the owner was selling the property. Did we get angry? No. Were we frustrated? Yes. We didn't share this news with the congregation.

After a couple of months, I searched the website to see if the property was yet listed. When I saw that it was, I called the realtor again. She was surprised to hear I wanted to try again. After further research, she informed me that other offers were made on the building, but none sparked the seller's interest. I did something I never did before. I petitioned God for the unthinkable. A wise man once said, "In order to get something you've never had, you have to do something you've never done." That was my mission. I told her that this time around, the seller would be interested because we were going to make an offer they couldn't refuse. It would start with my unusual down payment.

After days of making *my* "down payments" of fasting and praying to Him, He gave me confirmation that He would take care of *the* down payment we needed for the building. Without questioning how, when, or where, I went to the bank and updated the address on our checks to reflect the address of the property. At this time, I had not told my husband anything. My next act of crazy faith required him to know what I had been up to. So, I shared with him that Landmark was going to have a new permanent location. He wanted to know the address. After I told him, he didn't stop me; he only asked how much of a down payment we had and how much we needed. I said, "Don't worry about that." His eyes grew wide as if he believed I had a sizeable cash-down payment. God gave me a blank check full of faith!

Our church anniversary was fast approaching. Edriece and I had the graphic designer make our programs with the address of the new property. Before she printed over a hundred copies, she asked if there were a mistake in the address. We said, "No." She put two and two together and congratulated us, not knowing that we were acting solely in faith.

NO ORDINARY COMPENSATION

The realtor called and informed us that the seller accepted our counteroffer, including unique monthly payments and a special down payment. The only thing left for us to have was the money to put down. The realtor asked if we would have it within thirty days. We were shy of nearly ten thousand dollars.

Someone I knew was in a bad car accident and requested prayer. Within weeks of my husband and I praying for her, God not only healed her body but granted her a sizeable compensation that helped her purchase a new vehicle and make updates to her home. I cried and rejoiced with her. Someone commented, "You're acting as if it were you." I replied, "Hey, the Bible said to rejoice with those who rejoice. I know if He did it for her, He can do it for me!" No sooner than I said that, it happened for me.

I usually hit the "no receipt" button whenever I visit the ATM. On this day, I requested the receipt after I made my withdrawal. I had to do a double take when I saw the remaining balance. I immediately praised God! Because it was a weekend and the bank was closed, I pulled off to the side to look at my account information using my mobile app. I saw that the remaining balance was correct. My account reflected a deposit from the Department of Veteran Affairs for retroactive compensation due to my assault in the Army.

I promised the Lord that I would put it towards the down payment of the church. My husband wanted to know if I were sure. He knew I had been through so much and felt I was owed the money, but I hadn't been more sure in my life. After I did, I had about a thousand dollars left. I divided it up and used it to be a blessing to every individual who played a part in helping me pursue my case.

NO ORDINARY WINDOW

The clock was ticking. We had less than a week to be out of our current building. This was no ordinary window. As usual, we didn't panic. Unlike usual, our realtor asked the seller if we could move all of our things into the new building before closing. The seller was gracious enough to grant us the space, given our special circumstances. We only needed help packing and moving. God sent on help.

NO ORDINARY OPENING

My family and I put in serious work to make the church a clean and beautiful place of worship. This time, my husband's work hours wouldn't allow him to work alongside me. Therefore, I would start various projects like painting, and he would finish them. I would do the dirty work of cleaning out the attic, storage room, and restrooms, but he would do the hard work of hauling heavy items to the curb or traveling to various destinations to fix or replace sinks and appliances. It was definitely a team effort. Each day, God sent someone to help in areas where we needed assistance.

We waited two months before announcing our grand opening. It was exciting to know so many people were rooting for us. On a windy Sunday afternoon, family and friends came to witness the ribbon-cutting ceremony.

NO ORDINARY PLANT (LIFE) (PHOTOSYNTHESIS)

On opening day, a beautiful plant with a blue ribbon was delivered to the church along with a check and card. It was from our realtor. We had gifted her a check to thank her for her hard work and persistence in obtaining our church. She returned it with instructions that read: "You guys are good people. Please put the check towards your church's emergency stash. Best wishes."

We placed the plant in the foyer, where it grew and blossomed. When the winter months came, the plant slowly began to die. One person suggested repotting it; another recommended we take it down to our fellowship hall, where it was warmer. Doing so sucked the little life it had left. Eventually, they said, "It's time to throw it away." My husband also agreed that we let it go, but I couldn't bring myself to do it. I pleaded, "Give me one more chance to try something. If it doesn't work, you have my consent to pitch it." That was on a Saturday.

The next day, I poured some "blessed oil" (Extra Virgin Olive Oil that was prayed over) into a spray bottle of water. After pruning and ridding the plant of all the dead stems, I sprayed the leaves. By the time I finished, the plant had looked malnourished. What I did next nearly gave my husband a heart attack. I placed it in the sanctuary on top of the organ's speakers. Edriece said, "Girl, that is gonna distract me when I preach." I asked him to trust me.

That Wednesday for Bible Study, I went straight downstairs to help set up and start. My sons usually go to the sanctuary to bring down bibles for those who need them. Before I began, my boys ran up to me, yelling, "Mom! The plant is back alive!"

Everyone rushed to the sanctuary to see what all the fuss was about. My boys were correct. God has revived the plant and blessed it to blossom. I screamed, "I KNEW IT!" Then I asked, "Do y'all know why? It's because it was sitting under *The Son*. It wasn't long before it blossomed back to its original glory. We all rejoiced, knowing that if God can do it for a plant, He could do the same for anyone.

2 Thousand Twenty

NO ORDINARY VIRUS

"Jesus said unto her, I am the resurrection, and the life: he that believeth in me, though he were dead, yet shall he live."

— (JOHN 11:25-26) —

One day, while sitting at the dinner table with my family, my daughter asked me the most unusual question: "Mom, how do I know if God is real?" Looking at it from a parental perspective, I said, "Girl, how do you *not* know?" It led to a discussion that ended with her saying, "I know what you all say, but I want my own experience with God."

It was true. She had never had a personal encounter with God. It was I who witnessed the miracles of God in my family. I saw Him bless her to undergo open-heart surgery at six days old. I was there to see my husband walk away from a horrible car accident that totaled his vehicle. I experienced my youngest son survive being electrocuted at school in kindergarten. And I watched my oldest son walk away with stitches after nearly getting mauled by a Pit Bull. Now, it was their turn to develop a deeper relationship with God and witness His almighty hand over my life. This was the year God revived me.

March 10, 2020, an executive order was issued by the Department of Health and Human Services after identifying the first two probable cases of the coronavirus (Covid-19) in Michigan. We were instructed to reduce the size of local gatherings to fifty as a safety measure.

March 14, 2020, I had a previously planned women's event at my church. At this time, there was no mask mandate. We kept sanitizer and encouraged frequent hand washing. It was a powerful celebration.

March 23, 2020, another executive order was issued to help suppress the spread of Covid-19. The order directed residents to remain at home and stay safe.

March 24, 2020, I had flu-like symptoms. My body was achy, and I had chills. I called my family doctor, who suggested I come to the office but remain in my car to get tested for the flu. I found out that it was actually a Covid-19 test. I awaited the results. After three days with no answer, my situation worsened. I tossed and turned, trying to find relief for hours. I couldn't eat.

March 26, 2020, at approximately 11:00 at night, I could barely breathe. I tried crawling to the bathroom. When I made it there, I beckoned for my husband to try finding me something to wear to take me to the hospital. He was reluctant because he had heard on the news that the hospitals were sending people home if cases weren't severe. In the few serious cases, not many patients made it out alive. I insisted that something was wrong and that I needed to go.

He picked out something in my closet I hadn't worn in decades, complete with socks and church shoes. I wanted to ask, "Of all things, this is what you found that stood out to you?" However, I was too weak. I smiled and whispered, "Thank you, Honeybear," while he went to warm up the car. My children were asleep, so I didn't wake them to say, "See you later." I did tell my mother.

Edriece waited for me at the door and walked me to the car. Every step was a fight for strength and air. I could tell by the look on his face that he wasn't happy. He hardly uttered a word in the car. When I noticed that he was heading towards Hurley Medical Center (which was much closer in distance), I touched his hand and whispered, "Genesys." This time, God had other plans. Genesys was about ten miles away. It would take approximately 15 minutes in light travel to arrive there. He was stern in saying, "Uh uh. If I'm taking my wife to the hospital, it's gonna be Hurley." By this time, I couldn't even whisper. With tears down my face, I pointed for him to keep driving in the direction of Genesys.

Getting admitted was a blur. I remember being asked the same questions my doctor asked: Are you running a fever? Do you have any underlying issues? Do you have a cough? Have you traveled outside the country in the past thirty days? Have you been around anyone exposed to Covid? I shook my head, "No" in each case. I asked if my husband was coming in. The nurse said, "Honey, your husband can't come in." The moment she said that tears streamed down my face. When it comes to my husband, I'm a big baby. It was comforting when the nurse assured me it was for his own safety as she wheeled me to my room.

Minutes before midnight, I tested positive for Covid-19. The nurse handed me a hospital gown to change into and asked if I needed anything. I needed help getting into the gown. Next, she handed me my phone so I could tell my husband the news. He was still waiting in the hospital parking lot. I told him he could go home and asked if he could let my mom know. Everything after that was a blur.

*Please note: The next few paragraphs are based on what was shared with me **after** I came to or what I remembered subconsciously.*

March 27, 2020, I was intubated and put in an induced coma. Doing so allowed my heart and lungs to rest in order to heal.

For days, I dreamed I was in a restful place with a light above a door. I had a choice to stay asleep or follow my family into the light. I chose the light.

April 6, 2020, I opened my eyes. Above the door, in the room I was confined in, was a bright light in the shape of a cross. When I saw it, tears filled my eyes. When the blurriness faded away, I saw people that looked like minions. They wore yellow protective gear, blue face masks, large goggles, gloves, and black boots. I instantly thought, *"I've been kidnapped, and they're using me as a guinea pig."* I tried to talk but couldn't. I tried to move but couldn't.

"Darlin', are we happy to see you!" the team of minions applauded. "You've been under sedation for nearly two weeks now, and we were rooting for you to pull through!"

They began asking me questions to which I didn't know the answers, like where I was or why I was there.

"Honey, you are at Ascension. You were in a bad state after testing positive for Covid. We are your care team."

NO ORDINARY PATIENT

I scanned the room for my clothes and cell phone as soon as they left. I found neither of them. Suddenly, I remembered my dream. There, above my door, was a cross. I had to do a double take. I worked hard to remove the cuffs from around my legs. It was difficult to do with an IV in my dominant arm and another large cuff around my other arm. Yet, I didn't let it stop me. I must've triggered an alarm when I tried to get them off because my bed buzzed and flashed blue warning lights saying, "FALL RISK. DO NOT GET UP. I REPEAT, FALL RISK. DO NOT GET UP!"

One of the minions burst in the door and yelled, "WHAT ARE YOU DOING? YOU CAN NOT WALK! ARE YOU TRYING TO HURT YOURSELF?"

I shook my head. "No." After I whimpered in frustration, she said, "I know Darlin'. This is probably all confusing to you, but I will do my best to help you through it. In the meantime, I need to put these cuffs back around your legs. They help with circulation and prevent blood clots from forming. Now, I need you to behave and get some rest. If you need me, just press this red button for the nurse. Okay?" I agreed. Still, I couldn't get any rest. Time stood still.

I waited for what seemed like an hour to press the red call button. "Is everything okay," the nurse asked.

My eyes grew wide, and I shook my head. "No." I tried hard to believe that she was a nurse instead of a minion under orders to trick me.

"Before I go, I'll try to figure out what you want. Maybe I can say something, and you can point."

Everything she pointed to wasn't it. I didn't want the box of tissue. I didn't want an extra blanket; I was hot enough. I was trying to tell her I wanted my cell phone. She thought I wanted water.

"Oh no, Sweetie. You can't have any water. You were just extubated!"

"Exti-what?"

Water did sound like a good idea right about now, though. When she said I couldn't even have ice cubes, that was depressing. She did bring a soft spongy stick to help brush my teeth. When she stuck it in my mouth, I clamped down on it and sucked as much water as I could out of it.

"Let go, Honey. I have to brush your teeth and tongue. Are you gonna play nice?"

I nodded, "Yes."

When she returned after rinsing the spongy toothbrush, I sucked the water out of it again. I looked forward to getting my teeth brushed every shift change.

In her hand, she had a marker but didn't have time to get me something to write on. I touched her hand in order to put her ear close to my bedside. I gave it all I had to whisper the word "ph-oooo-ne."

"Honey, your phone is dead, and you can't talk yet. If you're trying to reach your husband, he just called. He's been calling every day. I updated him on your status. I'll look for you a charger."

Hearing that Edriece was calling every day was the sweetest sound to my ears. I missed him terribly. I know I said it before, but I can't stress it enough. I needed him. I wanted his touch. Being in the hospital was one thing. Being without him was heartbreaking.

The nurse came back with two chargers that were for an iPhone. They were useless for my Android. For a split second, I almost wished I had an iPhone for the sole purpose of having a charged phone. But, as soon as the thought entered my mind, I thought about all the cool things my Note 10 could do.

The next nurse reached out to my husband, who had brought my charger to the hospital in a plastic bag. After disinfecting, the nurse brought it to my room and charged my phone. I lit up like a Christmas tree. I couldn't wait for it to get some battery juice. I tried not to, but I soon fell asleep. Whenever I closed my eyes, I fought hard to separate reality from dreamland. Subconsciously, I made video and phone calls to my mom, sister, and a few friends.

NO ORDINARY NEWS

On April 8, 2020, my nurse told me she had some good news for me. "Guess what? You get to move out of ICU and onto the Covid floor. That's a good thing. You're one lucky gal." I knew luck had nothing to do with it, but I appreciated her enthusiasm. "You look amazing," she continued. I didn't feel amazing. I looked twice my age. My skin was dry and dark. I had lost so much weight and muscle. My legs looked like chopsticks and felt like Ramen Noodles.

Nurses were clapping, smiling, and crying as I left the ICU and arrived on the new floor. They were genuinely happy for me. I felt as though I should be clapping for them. Every day, they risked their lives to care for me and many other patients. Two nurses, in particular, went to great lengths to literally help me get back on my feet. They crushed my medication and put it in applesauce to help me swallow it better; they spoon-fed me, bathed me, lotioned my legs, hands, and feet, brushed my teeth and hair, kept my lips moisturized with ChapStick, and encouraged me to fight.

April 10, 2020, one of the nurses asked me if I had someone at home that could help take care of me. I said, "YES!" After that, a team of doctors came in and evaluated me. By now, my oxygen levels were much better, I was talking slightly better, and I could hold my eating utensils and toothbrush. They were pleased with my progress. Before the chief physician left, he asked me the question I'd wanted to know for days: "Are you ready to go home?" I replied with the largest grin and nodded, "Yes!"

The nurse returned to take out my IV and all the other tubes attached to my arm and chest to keep me alive.

"Do me a favor," she asked. "Do not look when I take out this device. Some people pass out when they see how long it is."

It took her forever to get the tape off, especially with surgical gloves on. When I was given the cue, I turned away. Boy, am I glad I did. After that, she prepped me for discharge by removing everything else.

Next, I was ready to attempt to freshen up. I used my IV stand to balance myself to walk to the restroom. After washing my face and brushing my teeth, I styled my hair. It took me two hours, but I was ready to go home. I asked if my husband needed to be informed. They told me I would be transported in a medical vehicle since I couldn't quite walk yet. That was even better. It gave me an opportunity to surprise my family. Unfortunately, I misunderstood the conversation.

The Medstar vehicle passed the exit for my house. When I asked the assistant driver if they knew my address, she replied, "We're not taking you home. Before you can go home, you must first go to rehab."

"The facility you're going to is in Frankenmuth." I felt hoodwinked, bamboozled, led astray, run amok, and flat-out deceived! Why would the doctors or nurses give me false hope after all I had been through?

"Welcome to Medilodge of Frankenmuth," the woman said. "I don't know if they told you, but this is a lockdown facility – no visitors in and none out. It's for your safety and ours. Let me show you to your room."

Frankenmuth was the nearest available facility for Covid patients. She took me down a long hallway. It reminded me of the military barracks I stayed in while stationed in Georgia. Needless to say, I was not thrilled. I felt my adrenaline pumping. I had to pull out one of the breathing devices prescribed to me by Ascension to help me take deep breaths to prevent having an anxiety attack.

"Here you go," the woman said as she handed me a coloring book, colored pencils, baby oil, baby wash, lip balm, and footies. "These should help keep you busy during the weeks you're here with us."

I couldn't think about weeks.

"Here's a walker for when you need to go to the restroom, and here's the TV remote. Before I forget, dinner will be served around 7:00. Should you need anything else, just press this button. Someone will be down as soon as they can."

I murmured the words, "I want to go home. I want my husband. Lord, I need to be with him. I... can't... breathe... without him." I repeated them until I gasped for air.

As I lay looking up at the ceiling, I realized I had it all wrong. God wanted me to long for *Him*. He wanted me to need more of *Him*.

I praised God, saying, "Lord, I can't breathe without YOU! I can't live without YOU! I miss YOU. I thank You for another chance to live for YOU! I want more of YOU! I vow to use this new lease on life to be Your mouthpiece. I vow to come out different—to grow wiser, stronger, and deeper in YOU.

On April 11, 2020, I discovered another person close to me had passed away. It hit even harder because he was someone I had known for years. He even sang at my tenth-anniversary vow renewal. And days before having Covid, he had asked if I could do him a favor. In return, he told me that he would hook my eyebrows up. We laughed together. It hurt so bad, especially because he was younger than me. After I prayed for his family, I did my best to stay positive. I did so by Facetiming my family and drawing in the coloring books the nurse had given me. It helped pass the time because I still hadn't gotten my hand coordination back. When I finally finished one page, I tore it out of the book and tacked it to the small bulletin board in my room.

April 12, 2020, my husband sent me a link to download an app called Zoom. It was new, but it allowed me to see him. The next day, I could see him and everyone in our church group. It was nice seeing everyone though not all understood that I couldn't quite talk yet. I appreciated my husband for including me.

April 13, 2020, I began physical therapy. My routine consisted of lifting a weight bar, hand-and-eye coordination by stacking cups, learning how to get up from the bed using the walker, and walking to the door of my room. Each task was used to strengthen my muscles in preparation for returning home—the most challenging being walking.

Each day, I stretched a little wider, stood a little longer, and walked a little further until I was allowed to walk in the hallway. I couldn't help thinking, *"If I were just a tad bit stronger, I could escape out of the emergency door exit."* But, who was I kidding? I would be caught within minutes of passing out on the grass. It looked so peaceful and free on the other side of the door.

Before long, I was going to the bathroom on my own and bathing myself. I was later approved for receiving ice chips and finally water.

Every day before doing anything, I talked to God first. I set daily goals and reminders to read scripture, pray, and hear from God. I listened to my mom, who stayed optimistic about my recovery journey.

My speech never fully recovered from being on the ventilator. But, given time, I knew I would get better. And I did. Calling home was enjoyable. Seeing how many people were praying for me became inspiring. Watching our virtual services was lifting. Before long, I was given the news I'd waited weeks to receive.

"Mrs. Lynn, it looks like you'll be able to go home in a few days. How's that sound?"

It sounded like heaven to me.

April 23, 2020, I woke up packed and ready to go home. When my phone rang, I could tell by the ring tone that it was a Facetime call. On the other end was my handsome husband. He had the largest smile on his face. When he saw me, he said, "Hey, Pretty Girl!" That was all I needed to hear. From there, he wanted to know all the information to pick me up.

The nurses told me I would be discharged at 2:00 p.m. It seemed so far away from 7:00 a.m. as I finished breakfast. I tried taking a nap. It didn't work. I tried coloring. It was a no-go. I even tried watching television, but I was too anxious. At 1:00 p.m., I was given a ton of paperwork. Most of it was a formality and making sure I had someone in place to help care for me. Finally, I was released to go home.

Outside, my husband waited for me with open arms. I wanted to cry as I hugged his neck, but he wore my favorite cologne and smelled too good for me to be sorrowful.

I looked around for his car and couldn't find it. He'd driven up in my new car and rubbed it in my face. We smiled and held hands as we drove off the lot. Before we merged onto the freeway, I asked him if he could pull over for a second. He looked puzzled. I didn't need to explain when he saw the look on my face.

I cried, "THANK YOU, LORD!!!!!!!!!!!!!!!!! I THANK YOU FOR MY LIFE!"

Afterward, I went live on Facebook to share the news. It didn't matter that I didn't look like myself or that my voice sounded like a harmonica whenever I got excited. I was alive and wanted the world to know.

Everything looked different. It all looked new, even my home.

My mother waited at the front door with two signs in her hands. One read, "Welcome home, Lady Lynn." In the living room awaited my children, ready to give me the largest bear hug they could give.

My oldest son waited on his dad's nod to "cue the music." He played "Forever" by Jason Nelson. If you've learned anything about me by this point, you can pretty much guess what I did next.

The next few weeks were a struggle. Having my family help me was more than I had ever witnessed. No one complained. They felt honored to lend a helping hand. Even extended family did what they could to ensure we lacked nothing.

Weeks later, I was able to share my testimony on various media outlets, including Flintside, ABC Channel 12 News, and SCARS Uplift Association.

May 31, 2020, the state of Michigan reported 57,397 confirmed cases and 5,491 deaths from the coronavirus. I could've been number 5,492. But God! What was meant to kill me actually birthed an entirely new me.

On June 10, 2020, I received a bill summary totaling $298,561.73, including my time in the hospital and rehab. I burst into tears and cried, "LORD, YOU THOUGHT I WAS WORTH SAVING!"

2 Thousand Twenty-One

— NO ORDINARY KICK —

*"...with men this is impossible; but with
God all things are possible."*

— [MATTHEW 19:26] —

Sometimes it can feel as if life has kicked you in the butt. It turns you left when you're trying to go right, brings you down as you reach towards the top, and pulls you back in when you press to move forward. It's not easy, but with God's direction, it's achievable. After making it over one hurdle, this was the year God blessed me to get over the next one.

NO ORDINARY TEST

I had a menstrual cycle that lasted for nearly four months. Afterward, my cycles were inconsistent. It raised some concerns. Following the check-up visit, my doctor sent me to a diagnostic clinic to get a second opinion on some test results.

I was told that it could be cancerous or require surgery. I prayed, my husband prayed, and a select group of women I shared the news with prayed. Prayer definitely changed things. The results were noncancerous, and things went back to normal after two minor surgeries.

The bloodwork at my follow-up appointment was no ordinary assessment, especially during a pandemic. My husband had driven me but had to stay in the car. I was required to wear a mask and answer a series of questions: "Have you or anyone you've been in contact with experienced any Covid symptoms? Have you traveled outside the country? Have you tested for Covid in the last three weeks?

When the nurse returned to the room, I couldn't believe my eyes and ears. "Mrs. Lynn, everything came back fine. We also have great news: your bloodwork shows high levels of HCG. Congratulations on your pregnancy!

I wanted to tell the whole world, but I would have to wait. Every time a "what if" or an ounce of doubt entered my mind, I blocked it with praise. I became so confident in what God was going to do that I purchased my very first baby item ever – a diaper bag. I could've bought gender-neutral items, but God had revealed to me in a dream that I was having a girl. In the dream, she was healthy and resting in her daddy's arms. It was comforting.

Week after week, we experienced scares of unwanted news. Each time, God reminded me: "Don't let what you *see* make you forget what I *said*."

During the last "scare," I was able to hear the baby's strong heartbeat and see the baby move. It was an indescribable feeling. I decided then to begin making a journal of all the dates and events to share with the baby to remember.

At my 35-week follow-up appointment, I mentioned to my team of doctors that my headaches had returned. I also showed him my super swollen ankles. Since my blood pressure was considered normal, I was told to monitor things. When I came in for my 36-week checkup and fetal monitoring, I had a headache, swollen legs, and rosy cheeks. I was sent to the ER immediately after reading my blood pressure results, where they told me I had preeclampsia. After three days of trying to lower my blood pressure, I was scheduled for surgery to deliver.

Other than the many scares, I had an overall good pregnancy. I couldn't help but thank God we finished getting the baby's room ready, complete with her crib and changing table that her brothers helped put together. In fact, for everything that came in the mail (whether we purchased them or they were gifted to us), my boys were Johnny-On-the-Spot, ensuring their soon-to-arrive sister was squared away. The added touches were the beautiful pink velvet rocking chair from my mother-in-law and the lovely wall art painted by my daughter Imari that spelled out the name "Ella."

My husband was able to get time off early to be with me during my stay in the ER. We were sure to pray fervently each day and night, informing our family of any updates.

Our little princess was the smallest of all our children and arrived earlier than the rest. She came out crying like me. I was too nauseous to nurse her, but I gave it my best shot. She wanted to stay snuggled up the entire time. I didn't mind. I had waited fourteen years and nine months for her arrival.

This time around, I vowed to take my time and enjoy motherhood (the waking up in the middle of the night to nurse, entertain, change diapers, and repeat). Through it all, having this heaven-sent blessing has made a tremendous difference in my life and the lives of many others. It hasn't been a walk in the park starting over in the parenting game, but it has been doable with our village of family, friends, and neighbors.

2 Thousand and...

NO ORDINARY STORY

"And the LORD turned the captivity of Job, when he prayed for his friends: also the LORD gave Job twice as much as he had before... So the LORD blessed the latter end of Job more than his beginning..."

— [JOB 42:10-12A] —

Someone once said I would tell my story of how I overcame all the things life had thrown at me, and it would become part of someone else's survival guide. That is my prayer for every reader.

I accepted that my life is my story, and no one else can tell it better than me. I'm no ordinary soldier! All the things God allowed me to experience may not have felt good, but they worked out for my good. I'm no ordinary soldier!

My "Golden Rule of Literature" is to never judge a book by its cover. When looking at me, people may not know that I struggled to get where I am. They won't know by looking at me that I have an unordinary testimony, an unordinary cover, or an unordinary story. They would have to learn that I serve an extraordinary God who gives me unordinary strength and an unordinary faith. I'm no ordinary soldier!

In the story of my life, God had to close the curtains to set me up for the next scene. He had already proved in the previous years that He could flip the script. I finally understand that bad chapters can still create wonderful stories. The ugliest parts of my story ended up being the most powerful elements of my testimony. Whether people choose to leave my life/story or if I have to leave and move on to the next chapter knowing they would no longer be in it, God helped me realize that their departure is not the end of my story. It was just the end of their part in it. I'm no ordinary soldier!

This book alone cannot hold what He has done, what He is doing now, and what He has yet to do in my life. The best thing is that He is not through blessing me. I know because I am still here to tell it. The best is yet to come for me. I'm no ordinary soldier!

Ordinary people read a book from beginning to end. They finish one chapter, close it, and begin the next chapter. I encourage you as I encourage myself to see yourself in the future. Continue turning the page, knowing God has some pretty awesome things in store for you. You're no ordinary soldier!